Embedded Systems with C

Programming Microcontrollers for Real-World Applications Develop firmware and real-time applications using C

THOMPSON CARTER

TABLE OF CONTENTS

Introduction

Embedded Systems with C: Programming Microcontrollers for Real-World Applications

Embedded systems are at the heart of the modern technological landscape, powering everything from consumer electronics and industrial machinery to medical devices and automobiles. These systems, which are designed to perform specific tasks within larger systems, are becoming increasingly sophisticated, enabling devices to interact intelligently with their environments, process data in real-time, and communicate over networks. As the world becomes more connected, the demand for embedded systems is growing, and developers need to stay ahead of the curve to build efficient, reliable, and scalable solutions.

"Embedded Systems with C: Programming Microcontrollers for Real-World Applications" is a comprehensive guide to understanding and developing embedded systems, focusing on practical applications using the C programming language. This book is designed for both beginners and experienced developers who want to dive deeper into the world of embedded systems, offering a detailed, hands-on approach to building real-world embedded applications.

Why Embedded Systems Matter

Embedded systems are everywhere. From smartphones to smart thermostats, drones to industrial robots, embedded systems form the backbone of nearly every modern electronic device. Unlike general-purpose computers, embedded systems are tailored to perform a specific set of tasks and are optimized for real-time processing, energy efficiency, and low cost. This makes them indispensable for applications where high performance, low power consumption, and reliability are critical.

Embedded systems are often constrained by resources, such as limited memory, processing power, and storage. As a result, developers must optimize both hardware and software to meet these constraints while still delivering robust functionality. The programming of these systems requires a unique set of skills and knowledge, especially when it comes to interfacing with hardware, managing real-time requirements, and ensuring system stability.

Why C Programming for Embedded Systems?

C has long been the language of choice for embedded systems development. Its combination of low-level hardware access, efficiency, and portability makes it an ideal fit for programming microcontrollers and other embedded hardware. Unlike high-level languages, C allows developers to directly manipulate memory, control hardware registers, and manage timing—all of which are essential for embedded system development.

While modern programming languages offer higher-level abstractions, C remains relevant for embedded systems because it provides precise control over system resources. It is also highly efficient, which is crucial for systems that operate under tight resource constraints. Furthermore, many embedded development environments, including popular microcontroller platforms like **Arduino**, **STM32**, and **ESP32**, rely heavily on C for programming their chips.

In this book, we focus on using C to program microcontrollers for real-world embedded applications. By using C, developers can gain a deeper understanding of how their code interacts with hardware, allowing them to write more efficient and reliable embedded software.

What You'll Learn

This book takes you on a journey from understanding the fundamental concepts of embedded systems to building your own fully functional embedded applications. It covers key topics such as:

- **Basic Concepts of Embedded Systems**: Understanding the core principles of embedded systems, their components, and their unique challenges.
- **Microcontroller Architecture and Components**: Learn how microcontrollers work, including the CPU, memory, and peripherals, and how they interact with external devices.
- **Programming in C for Embedded Systems**: Master the C language with an emphasis on embedded-specific features such as memory management, hardware access, and real-time constraints.
- **Interfacing with Sensors and Actuators**: Learn how to connect sensors (e.g., temperature, motion, pressure) and actuators (e.g., motors, relays) to your embedded system and control them through software.
- **Communication Protocols**. Understand how to use common communication protocols like UART, SPI, and I2C to interface with external devices and systems.

- **Real-Time Operating Systems (RTOS)**: Explore how real-time operating systems manage tasks in embedded systems and how to develop multitasking applications.
- **Power Management**: Learn techniques for reducing power consumption in battery-powered embedded systems.
- **Debugging and Testing Embedded Systems**: Understand the tools and techniques for debugging embedded applications and ensuring they work reliably under real-world conditions.
- **Security in Embedded Systems**: Gain insights into securing embedded systems, including data encryption, authentication, and secure boot.
- **Building Complete Embedded Applications**: Put everything together by developing a real-world application from start to finish, including hardware design, software development, and testing.

Real-World Applications

Throughout the book, we use practical examples and case studies to demonstrate the concepts discussed. You'll learn how to build actual applications, such as a **smart thermostat**, **smart home devices**, and **industrial automation systems**, using real-world hardware. These applications are designed to show how embedded systems are used in everyday devices and industrial settings, providing a hands-on approach to understanding the intricacies of embedded systems.

By the end of this book, you will have the skills to:

- Design, program, and deploy embedded systems for a variety of applications.
- Interface microcontrollers with sensors, actuators, and external devices.
- Apply real-time techniques to manage timing and resource constraints.
- Optimize power consumption for battery-powered systems.
- Implement security measures in embedded systems.

Who This Book Is For

This book is aimed at:

- **Beginners**: Those new to embedded systems programming or C who want to understand the principles of embedded systems and how to build them.
- **Experienced Programmers**: Developers with experience in C programming or general-purpose computing who want to learn how to apply their skills to embedded systems.

- **Engineers and Designers**: Hardware engineers and systems designers who want to expand their knowledge of embedded software development.
- **IoT Developers**: Developers building Internet of Things (IoT) devices who need to understand how to program low-power, real-time embedded systems.

Preparing for the Future of Embedded Systems

The field of embedded systems is rapidly evolving, driven by trends like the **Internet of Things (IoT)**, **edge computing**, and **artificial intelligence (AI)**. Embedded systems are becoming smarter, more interconnected, and more capable of processing complex tasks. As the demand for smart devices grows, there is an increasing need for developers who can design systems that are efficient, reliable, and scalable.

This book not only provides the technical knowledge needed to develop embedded systems using C but also prepares you for future developments in the field. You'll learn how to approach new challenges, adapt to emerging technologies, and design embedded systems that are ready for the future.

Conclusion

"Embedded Systems with C: Programming Microcontrollers for Real-World Applications" is your gateway to mastering embedded systems development. With practical examples, hands-on projects, and a focus on real-world applications, this book provides you with the tools and knowledge to design and implement embedded systems that meet the needs of modern technology. Whether you're building your first embedded project or looking to deepen your expertise, this book will guide you step by step through the exciting world of embedded systems, preparing you for a successful career in embedded systems development.

CHAPTER 1

INTRODUCTION TO EMBEDDED SYSTEMS

Overview of Embedded Systems, Real-Time Applications, and Microcontrollers

Embedded systems are specialized computing systems designed to perform a dedicated function within a larger system. Unlike general-purpose computers, which can run a variety of applications, embedded systems are built to handle specific tasks, often with constraints such as limited resources, low power consumption, and real-time performance requirements.

These systems are used in a wide range of applications, including automotive control systems, medical devices, consumer electronics, and industrial automation. A key feature of embedded systems is their ability to interact with the physical world through sensors, actuators, and other hardware interfaces.

Real-time applications are systems that require responses within a specific time constraint. For instance, in a heart rate monitor, the system must read sensor data and provide feedback in real time to ensure accuracy and reliability. Real-time systems can be classified as hard or soft real-time. Hard real-time systems must meet their deadlines without exception (e.g., airbag deployment systems in cars), while soft real-time systems aim to meet deadlines most of the time, but occasional delays are tolerable (e.g., streaming video).

A **microcontroller** (MCU) is the heart of many embedded systems. It is a small computer on a single integrated circuit that includes a processor, memory, and I/O interfaces. Microcontrollers are often used in embedded systems due to their small size, low cost, and energy efficiency. They can be programmed to execute specific tasks based on the embedded system's requirements.

Key Differences Between General-Purpose Computing and Embedded Systems

1. **Purpose and Functionality**
   - **General-Purpose Computing**: A general-purpose computer, such as a desktop or laptop, is designed to handle a wide range of tasks. It can run multiple applications concurrently, such as word processing, gaming, and internet browsing.

   - **Embedded Systems**: In contrast, embedded systems are designed to perform a specific function or set of functions. For example, a washing machine's embedded system controls the wash cycles and interfaces with the hardware components like the motor and sensors.

2. **Hardware and Software Flexibility**
   - **General-Purpose Computing**: These systems typically offer extensive hardware and software flexibility, allowing users to install and run a variety of software applications and make hardware upgrades.
   - **Embedded Systems**: The hardware in embedded systems is often fixed, and the software is tailored to the specific needs of the system. Modifying the software or hardware of an embedded system is typically more challenging.

3. **Resource Constraints**
   - **General-Purpose Computing**: These systems are designed to work with large amounts of memory, processing power, and storage. They can handle resource-intensive tasks, such as video editing or running complex simulations.
   - **Embedded Systems**: Embedded systems are usually resource-constrained, meaning they must function within strict limits for memory,

processing power, and energy consumption. For instance, an MCU in an embedded system may only have a few kilobytes of memory and a low clock speed.

4. **Real-Time Performance**
   - **General-Purpose Computing**: While general-purpose computers can multitask and handle multiple processes at once, they do not always guarantee real-time performance. They rely on operating systems that may introduce latency in handling tasks.
   - **Embedded Systems**: Real-time performance is often crucial for embedded systems. Whether it's a life-critical application like an airbag deployment system or an industrial robot's movement control, embedded systems often require deterministic and predictable behavior, where delays are unacceptable.
5. **Power Consumption**
   - **General-Purpose Computing**: These systems tend to consume significantly more power, as they are designed to perform a variety of tasks and often have large displays and additional hardware components.
   - **Embedded Systems**: Power consumption is a critical consideration for embedded systems,

particularly in battery-operated devices like portable medical devices or IoT sensors. These systems must be optimized for low power consumption while still performing their tasks effectively.

6. **Cost**
   - **General-Purpose Computing**: These systems typically cost more because of their versatile hardware and capabilities.
   - **Embedded Systems**: The components of embedded systems are generally more cost-effective, as they are purpose-built and optimized for specific tasks.

Understanding these differences is essential for anyone working with embedded systems, especially when designing systems with limited resources, real-time requirements, and specific tasks. By the end of this chapter, you'll have a foundational grasp of the unique characteristics that define embedded systems, preparing you for deeper exploration in the upcoming chapters.

CHAPTER 2

BASICS OF C PROGRAMMING FOR EMBEDDED SYSTEMS

Introduction to C Programming

C is one of the most widely used programming languages in embedded systems development. Its efficiency, flexibility, and ability to work directly with hardware make it the ideal choice for writing firmware and low-level software for embedded applications. C provides a balance between high-level abstractions and low-level memory management, offering developers the ability to write efficient code that can directly control hardware while being portable across different microcontroller platforms.

In embedded systems, C is used to write programs that interact directly with the microcontroller's hardware, such as reading from sensors, controlling actuators, and handling interrupts. Understanding the fundamentals of C programming is essential for anyone working in this field.

Here are the key aspects of C programming that are especially important for embedded systems:

1. **Low-Level Memory Access**
   C allows direct access to memory using pointers, which is critical for embedded systems that must manage memory efficiently. You can manipulate hardware registers, memory-mapped I/O, and stack frames to achieve real-time performance.
2. **Efficient Execution**
   Embedded systems often run on microcontrollers with limited processing power. C allows developers to write highly optimized code by controlling how instructions are executed and how memory is used, resulting in faster and smaller programs.
3. **Modularity and Reusability**
   C encourages the use of functions, structures, and libraries to modularize code, making it easier to reuse across different parts of a project or in future projects.
4. **Portability**
   While embedded systems are often hardware-specific, C provides the ability to write portable code. By following industry standards and writing modular code, embedded systems developers can port their applications to different microcontroller platforms with minimal changes.

Writing Your First C Program for an Embedded System

To get started, let's write a simple C program that will run on an embedded system. The program will toggle an LED connected to one of the microcontroller's GPIO pins, which is a common starting point for embedded systems development.

Step 1: Set Up the Development Environment

Before you can write and upload your program to a microcontroller, you need to set up the embedded development environment. This includes:

- **Compiler/IDE**: An Integrated Development Environment (IDE) such as MPLAB X (for Microchip PIC), STM32CubeIDE (for STM32), or Atmel Studio (for AVR) provides all the necessary tools for writing, compiling, and debugging C code for embedded systems.
- **Toolchain**: This includes the C compiler, linker, and other utilities required for embedded systems development. A popular toolchain for embedded systems is GCC (GNU Compiler Collection).
- **Hardware Interface**: To upload code to the microcontroller, you need a programmer/debugger (e.g., ST-Link for STM32, USBasp for AVR) and a connection to the target microcontroller.

Step 2: Writing the Code

Let's start with a simple LED toggle program. The LED will be connected to a GPIO pin on the microcontroller, and every time the program runs, the LED will switch from on to off.

Here's the basic structure of a C program for an embedded system:

c

```
#include <stdio.h>      // Standard input/output
header (optional, used for debugging)
#include <avr/io.h>         // Header for AVR
microcontroller (specific to the platform you are
using)
#include <util/delay.h> // Delay functions for
timing (if applicable)

#define LED_PIN 0        // Define the pin number
where the LED is connected (e.g., pin 0 on PORTB)

// Function to initialize the GPIO pin for the
LED
void init_LED(void) {
    DDRB |= (1 << LED_PIN);  // Set LED_PIN as an
output on PORTB
}
```

```
// Function to turn the LED on
void turn_on_LED(void) {
    PORTB |= (1 << LED_PIN);  // Set the LED_PIN
high to turn the LED on
}

// Function to turn the LED off
void turn_off_LED(void) {
    PORTB &= ~(1 << LED_PIN); // Set the LED_PIN
low to turn the LED off
}

// Main program loop
int main(void) {
    init_LED();  // Initialize the LED pin as an
output

    while(1) {   // Infinite loop for embedded
systems
        turn_on_LED();     // Turn on the LED
        _delay_ms(500);        // Wait for 500
milliseconds
        turn_off_LED();    // Turn off the LED
        _delay_ms(500);   // Wait for another 500
milliseconds
    }
    return 0;  // This line will never be reached
in embedded systems
```

```
}
```

Step 3: Explanation of the Code

1. **Includes**:
    - #include <avr/io.h> is specific to AVR microcontrollers (you'll need to adjust this depending on the microcontroller platform you're using). It provides access to the microcontroller's registers.
    - #include <util/delay.h> is used for the _delay_ms() function, which introduces a simple delay in the program.
2. **Pin Definition**:
    - #define LED_PIN 0 defines the GPIO pin number where the LED is connected (e.g., pin 0 of PORTB on an AVR microcontroller).
3. **Initialization**:
    - init_LED() configures the LED pin as an output by setting the corresponding bit in the data direction register (DDRB for AVR).
4. **Turn LED On/Off**:
    - turn_on_LED() sets the corresponding bit in the port register (PORTB for AVR) to make the pin high, turning on the LED.
    - turn_off_LED() clears the bit, turning the LED off.

5. **Main Loop**:
   - The `while(1)` loop runs indefinitely, alternating the LED on and off every 500 milliseconds, simulating a blinking LED.

Step 4: Compile and Upload the Code

Once you've written your program, you can compile it using your IDE's build tools, which will convert the C code into machine code that can be understood by the microcontroller. After compiling, you can upload the firmware to the microcontroller using a programmer/debugger.

Conclusion

Writing your first program for an embedded system is the first step toward mastering embedded C programming. As you progress, you will begin to interact with other peripherals, handle more complex tasks, and optimize your code for performance and resource constraints. In the following chapters, we will explore more advanced topics such as handling interrupts, managing memory, and interfacing with various sensors and communication protocols.

CHAPTER 3

EMBEDDED C ENVIRONMENT SETUP

Setting Up Development Tools: Compilers, IDEs, Debuggers

To start programming embedded systems with C, you need to set up a development environment that allows you to write, compile, and debug your code. The key components in this environment are the **compiler**, **IDE (Integrated Development Environment)**, and **debugger**. Let's explore these in more detail.

1. Compilers

A **compiler** is a tool that converts your high-level C code into machine-readable code that can be executed by the microcontroller. For embedded systems, you usually need a cross-compiler, which is a compiler that runs on your host system (such as a PC or laptop) but generates code that can run on a different architecture (such as an ARM, AVR, or PIC microcontroller).

Some popular compilers for embedded systems include:

- **GCC (GNU Compiler Collection)**: GCC is one of the most widely used compilers for embedded systems. It supports a variety of microcontroller architectures and is part of many toolchains.
    - **AVR-GCC**: For AVR microcontrollers (like those from Atmel, now Microchip).
    - **ARM-GCC**: For ARM-based microcontrollers (such as STM32, NXP, etc.).
- **Clang**: Another open-source compiler that is gaining popularity. It is known for its high performance and modern features.
- **KEIL (for ARM microcontrollers)**: KEIL is a popular proprietary compiler that supports ARM-based microcontrollers.

2. Integrated Development Environments (IDEs)

An **IDE** is a software application that provides a comprehensive environment for writing, debugging, and compiling embedded C code. It typically includes a code editor, compiler, debugger, and other tools to make development easier.

Some commonly used IDEs for embedded systems include:

- **Eclipse**: Eclipse is a popular, open-source IDE that can be used with various embedded systems. It supports multiple compilers, including GCC and ARM-GCC, through the use of plugins. Eclipse offers features like syntax highlighting, code completion, and a built-in debugger.
- **Atmel Studio**: Atmel Studio is tailored for Atmel (now Microchip) microcontrollers, providing an easy-to-use environment for developing embedded software.
- **STM32CubeIDE**: This is a development environment for STM32 microcontrollers. It integrates STM32CubeMX for configuration and initialization and provides a powerful IDE to develop and debug embedded applications.
- **MPLAB X IDE**: MPLAB X is used for developing software for Microchip's PIC and dsPIC microcontrollers. It is based on the open-source NetBeans IDE.

3. Debuggers

A **debugger** is essential for identifying and fixing errors in embedded code. Debuggers allow you to step through your program, inspect variables, and interact with the microcontroller to check that everything is working as expected.

- **JTAG Debugger**: JTAG is a standard debugging interface that allows low-level debugging on many microcontrollers. Tools like the ST-Link (for STM32), J-Link (for ARM), and USBasp (for AVR) provide JTAG debugging support.
- **SWD (Serial Wire Debug)**: A more compact debugging interface used by ARM-based microcontrollers. It offers similar functionality to JTAG but uses fewer pins and is often used in development boards.
- **GDB (GNU Debugger)**: GDB is a popular open-source debugger that is integrated into many IDEs. It allows you to step through code, set breakpoints, and inspect the program's state during execution.

4. Hardware Interface Tools

To load your compiled program onto the microcontroller, you'll need a way to communicate between your computer and the microcontroller's flash memory. This is usually done using a **programmer** or **debugger** that connects to the microcontroller's debug interface (e.g., JTAG, SWD, or USB). Some common tools include:

- **ST-Link**: Used for STM32 microcontrollers.
- **J-Link**: Popular for ARM-based microcontrollers.
- **USBasp**: Commonly used for AVR microcontrollers.
- **PICkit**: Used for Microchip's PIC microcontrollers.

Introduction to the Concept of Cross-Compiling

Cross-compiling refers to the process of compiling code on one platform (the host system, such as a PC or laptop) and generating machine code for a different platform (the target system, such as a microcontroller). This is essential in embedded systems development because the development environment (host) is typically far more powerful than the microcontroller (target) you are programming.

Here's how cross-compiling works in the context of embedded systems:

1. **Host System**: The computer or development environment where you write and compile your C code. This could be running on an operating system like Windows, macOS, or Linux.

2. **Target System**: The microcontroller or embedded device that will run your compiled code. This is typically a small, resource-constrained device that does not have a full operating system or the capability to compile code directly.
3. **Cross-Compiler**: The cross-compiler runs on the host system and generates machine code that is tailored for the target system's architecture. For example, when you write C code for an ARM-based microcontroller, you use an ARM-GCC compiler to generate ARM-compatible machine code.
4. **Toolchain**: A collection of tools (compiler, linker, debugger) used for building software for the target system. The cross-compiler is part of this toolchain, along with libraries that are compatible with the target microcontroller.

For example, to write and compile code for an STM32 microcontroller, you would typically:

1. Write the C code on your host machine (PC).
2. Use the ARM-GCC compiler to compile the code into machine code that the STM32 can execute.
3. Upload the generated binary file to the STM32 using a programmer (e.g., ST-Link).

Cross-compiling is essential for embedded systems development because the microcontrollers in embedded systems are not equipped with the necessary resources to compile and run software directly. The entire development process, including compiling, debugging, and uploading the code, takes place on a more powerful host system.

Conclusion

Setting up the development environment for embedded C programming involves selecting the right compiler, IDE, and debugger, as well as understanding how cross-compiling works to build software for microcontrollers. As you move forward with embedded systems development, having a well-configured environment will help you write, test, and debug your code more efficiently. In the following chapters, you will learn how to use these tools effectively to work with hardware interfaces, sensors, and communication protocols.

CHAPTER 4

MICROCONTROLLER ARCHITECTURE AND COMPONENTS

Understanding Microcontrollers and Their Components (CPU, Memory, Peripherals)

A **microcontroller** (MCU) is a small, integrated computing device designed to control embedded systems. It is a central element of most embedded applications and contains all the necessary components to perform specific tasks efficiently. Microcontrollers are typically programmed with firmware to execute predefined tasks like reading sensor data, processing signals, and controlling external hardware.

Let's explore the main components of a microcontroller in detail.

1. CPU (Central Processing Unit)

The **CPU** is the brain of the microcontroller. It executes instructions from the program (firmware) and coordinates the operations of the other components. In embedded systems, the CPU is optimized for specific tasks rather than the wide range of activities found in general-purpose computers.

- **Functionality**: The CPU interprets and executes the machine instructions stored in memory. It processes data, performs mathematical and logical operations, and manages communication between the various components of the microcontroller.
- **Clock Speed**: The CPU operates at a specific clock speed, measured in Hertz (Hz), which determines how quickly it can execute instructions. For example, a microcontroller with a clock speed of 16 MHz can process 16 million instructions per second.
- **Registers**: The CPU uses internal registers to temporarily store data that it is currently working with. These registers are fast, small storage units that hold data or addresses for quick access.

2. Memory

Microcontrollers typically feature a variety of memory types that serve different functions. Memory in a microcontroller is divided into three main categories:

- **ROM (Read-Only Memory)**: ROM is used to store the firmware or program code. It is non-volatile, meaning that it retains its data even when the power is turned off. In most microcontrollers, the firmware is programmed into flash memory, a type of ROM that can be reprogrammed.
- **RAM (Random Access Memory)**: RAM is used to store variables, temporary data, and intermediate results that the microcontroller needs while running the program. RAM is volatile, so its contents are lost when the power is turned off.
- **EEPROM (Electrically Erasable Programmable Read-Only Memory)**: EEPROM is used for storing small amounts of data that need to persist between reboots, such as device configurations, calibration data, or user settings. EEPROM is non-volatile and can be erased and rewritten electronically.

Memory management in a microcontroller is crucial because the available memory is often limited, and developers need to optimize the use of each type of memory to ensure efficient operation.

3. Peripherals

Peripherals are external devices or circuits that a microcontroller interacts with to perform specific tasks. These peripherals can be built into the microcontroller (internal peripherals) or connected externally via communication protocols (external peripherals).

Internal Peripherals: These are components embedded within the microcontroller chip itself and are often used for handling input and output (I/O) tasks. Some common internal peripherals include:

- **Timers**: Used to generate precise time delays or to measure the passage of time. Timers are often used for scheduling tasks or generating PWM (Pulse Width Modulation) signals to control motors or LEDs.
- **Analog-to-Digital Converter (ADC)**: Converts analog signals (such as temperature readings) into digital data that the CPU can process. Microcontrollers with ADCs are used to interface with sensors that produce analog outputs.

- **Digital-to-Analog Converter (DAC)**: Converts digital data back into analog signals. DACs are often used to control actuators like motors or speakers.
- **Serial Communication Interfaces**: Microcontrollers often include peripherals for serial communication, such as UART (Universal Asynchronous Receiver-Transmitter), SPI (Serial Peripheral Interface), and I2C (Inter-Integrated Circuit). These protocols are used to exchange data with other devices or systems.
- **PWM (Pulse Width Modulation)**: Used for controlling devices like motors or LED brightness. PWM allows you to adjust the power delivered to a component by varying the duty cycle of the pulse.

External Peripherals: These are devices or components connected to the microcontroller, typically via communication protocols. Some common external peripherals include:

- **Sensors**: These devices provide real-time data, such as temperature, humidity, or light levels. Microcontrollers often interface with sensors to gather information about the environment.

- **Actuators**: These devices execute actions based on instructions from the microcontroller. For example, motors, relays, and solenoids are types of actuators that a microcontroller can control.
- **Displays**: Microcontrollers often control output devices like LCD or OLED screens to display information to the user, such as sensor readings or system status.

4. I/O Ports

Microcontrollers have input/output (I/O) ports that allow communication with external devices. These ports are used to read data from sensors (input) and send data to actuators or displays (output). I/O pins can be configured as either **digital** (binary) or **analog** depending on the type of data they need to handle.

- **Digital I/O**: Digital pins can be set to a high or low voltage (usually 0V or 3.3/5V) to represent binary data (0 or 1). These pins can be used to turn LEDs on/off, read button presses, or communicate with other digital devices.
- **Analog I/O**: Analog pins can read or output voltage levels that vary continuously within a certain range.

These are used to interface with sensors that provide analog data, such as temperature sensors or potentiometers.

The Role of Microcontrollers in Embedded Systems

Microcontrollers play a central role in embedded systems because they are the "brain" of the system, providing processing power, memory, and control over various hardware components. They are designed to handle specific tasks efficiently and can operate autonomously for extended periods without human intervention.

Here are some key roles that microcontrollers play in embedded systems:

1. **Control and Coordination**: The microcontroller is responsible for managing and coordinating the system's activities. For instance, in a washing machine, the microcontroller controls the wash cycle, motor speeds, water temperature, and user interface.
2. **Signal Processing**: Microcontrollers process data from sensors (analog-to-digital conversion) and make decisions based on that data. For example, a temperature sensor in an air conditioner may send

data to the microcontroller, which then adjusts the compressor speed to maintain the desired temperature.

3. **Real-Time Operations**: Many embedded systems require real-time responses to stimuli. The microcontroller manages real-time tasks like responding to external inputs (e.g., a button press) or controlling actuators (e.g., turning a motor on/off).
4. **Communication**: Microcontrollers enable communication between different parts of the system. They can communicate with external devices (sensors, actuators, displays) or even other embedded systems via serial communication protocols like UART, I2C, or SPI.
5. **Low Power Operation**: Since many embedded systems are battery-powered or need to run for long periods without a power source, microcontrollers are designed to operate with low power consumption. They enter low-power states when idle and can be woken up to perform tasks as needed.
6. **Customization and Flexibility**: Microcontrollers can be programmed to execute custom firmware tailored to the specific needs of an embedded system.

This allows for high customization and flexibility in terms of functionality.

Conclusion

Microcontrollers are at the heart of embedded systems, providing the computational power, memory, and control interfaces needed to interact with the physical world. Understanding their architecture and components is crucial for designing efficient embedded systems. In this chapter, we've covered the basic components of microcontrollers, including the CPU, memory, peripherals, and I/O ports, and explored their roles in embedded systems. As you progress through the book, you'll learn how to program these components in C to build real-world applications.

CHAPTER 5

DIGITAL I/O IN EMBEDDED SYSTEMS

Working with GPIO Pins

General Purpose Input/Output (GPIO) pins are a fundamental component in most embedded systems. These pins can be configured as either input or output and are used to interact with external devices or components. They are called "general-purpose" because they can be configured for a wide range of tasks, such as reading signals from buttons, controlling LEDs, or interfacing with other digital devices.

Microcontrollers typically have multiple GPIO pins, each of which can be configured individually for different tasks. The way these pins behave—whether they act as inputs or outputs—is controlled through the microcontroller's internal registers.

Here's an overview of how GPIO pins work:

1. **Input Mode**: When a GPIO pin is configured as an input, it reads the digital signal (high or low) coming

from an external component, such as a sensor or switch.

   - **High (1)**: A voltage is applied to the pin, typically 3.3V or 5V, which the microcontroller reads as a logical high.
   - **Low (0)**: When the pin is connected to ground (0V), the microcontroller reads it as a logical low.

2. **Output Mode**: When a GPIO pin is set to output mode, the microcontroller can control the pin's voltage level. It can either output a high voltage (to turn on an LED or activate a relay) or a low voltage (to turn off the device).
   - **High (1)**: The pin outputs a voltage (typically 3.3V or 5V), which can drive external components.
   - **Low (0)**: The pin outputs 0V, turning off any connected components.

Configuring GPIO Pins

To use GPIO pins in an embedded system, you need to configure them as either input or output. This is done by setting specific bits in the **Data Direction Register (DDR)** and the **Port Register (PORT)** in most microcontrollers.

For example, let's say you're working with an AVR-based microcontroller (e.g., ATmega328p) and want to configure a pin as an output to control an LED. You'd typically follow these steps:

1. **Set the pin as an output**: You modify the corresponding bit in the DDR register (Data Direction Register). A bit value of `1` indicates that the pin will act as an output, while `0` means it will be an input.
2. **Write to the pin**: You modify the corresponding bit in the PORT register to set the pin's output state (high or low).

Here's an example of how you can configure and control GPIO pins for a simple task like turning an LED on and off:

```
c

#include <avr/io.h> // AVR microcontroller-specific header

#define LED_PIN 0 // Define the pin where the LED is connected (pin 0 of PORTB)

void init_GPIO() {
```

```
    DDRB |= (1 << LED_PIN);  // Set LED_PIN as an
output (1 means output in DDR)
}

void turn_on_LED() {
    PORTB |= (1 << LED_PIN); // Set LED_PIN high
(turn on the LED)
}

void turn_off_LED() {
    PORTB &= ~(1 << LED_PIN); // Set LED_PIN low
(turn off the LED)
}

int main() {
    init_GPIO();  // Initialize the GPIO pin as
output

    while (1) {
        turn_on_LED();  // Turn on the LED
        _delay_ms(500);   //   Wait   for   500
milliseconds
        turn_off_LED(); // Turn off the LED
        _delay_ms(500); // Wait for another 500
milliseconds
    }

    return 0;
}
```

Explanation:

- **DDRB**: This is the Data Direction Register for **PORTB**. Setting a bit in `DDRB` to `1` configures the corresponding pin as an output, while `0` would configure it as an input.
- **PORTB**: This is the Port Register for **PORTB**. By setting or clearing bits in `PORTB`, we can drive the corresponding pins high or low.
- The code repeatedly turns the LED on and off every 500 milliseconds, making it blink.

Reading and Writing Digital Signals in C

Reading and writing digital signals in embedded systems is straightforward. In the case of input, the microcontroller reads the voltage level of a GPIO pin and stores it in a variable. For output, the microcontroller sets the state of a GPIO pin, either to high or low.

Writing Digital Signals (Output Mode)

To write a digital signal (either high or low) to a GPIO pin, you simply set or clear the corresponding bit in the **PORT** register.

Example:

```c
PORTB |= (1 << LED_PIN);   // Set the pin high (turn on the LED)
PORTB &= ~(1 << LED_PIN); // Set the pin low (turn off the LED)
```

Reading Digital Signals (Input Mode)

To read the state of a GPIO pin (whether it's high or low), you check the corresponding bit in the **PIN** register. The **PIN** register provides the current state of the input pins. For instance, if a button is connected to a GPIO pin, you can read the state of the button to determine if it's pressed or not.

Example:

```c
if (PINB & (1 << BUTTON_PIN)) {
    // If the corresponding bit is set, the pin is high (button pressed)
} else {
    // If the corresponding bit is clear, the pin is low (button not pressed)
}
```

In this example, the program checks whether the `BUTTON_PIN` is high or low. If it's high, it indicates that the button has been pressed, and the code inside the `if` block will execute.

Practical Example: Reading a Button and Controlling an LED

Let's combine both input and output operations to create a simple program that turns on an LED when a button is pressed.

```c
#include <avr/io.h>
#include <util/delay.h>

#define BUTTON_PIN 1 // Assume the button is connected to pin 1 of PORTB
#define LED_PIN 0       // Assume the LED is connected to pin 0 of PORTB

void init_GPIO() {
    DDRB |= (1 << LED_PIN);  // Set LED_PIN as an output
    DDRB &= ~(1 << BUTTON_PIN); // Set BUTTON_PIN as an input
    PORTB |= (1 << BUTTON_PIN); // Enable pull-up resistor on BUTTON_PIN (optional)
}

int main() {
```

```
    init_GPIO();  // Initialize GPIOs

    while (1) {
        if (!(PINB & (1 << BUTTON_PIN))) {   //
Check if the button is pressed (low)
            PORTB |= (1 << LED_PIN);  // Turn on
the LED
        } else {
            PORTB &= ~(1 << LED_PIN); // Turn off
the LED
        }

        _delay_ms(100);    // Small delay to
debounce the button press
    }

    return 0;
}
```

Explanation:

- **DDRB |= (1 << LED_PIN)**: Configures the LED pin as an output.
- **DDRB &= ~(1 << BUTTON_PIN)**: Configures the button pin as an input.
- **PORTB |= (1 << BUTTON_PIN)**: Enables the internal pull-up resistor for the button pin. This ensures the pin reads high when the button is not pressed and low when it is pressed.

- **if (!(PINB & (1 << BUTTON_PIN)))**: Reads the button pin. If the button is pressed, the pin will be low (0V), and the LED will turn on. Otherwise, the LED will turn off.

Conclusion

Digital I/O is a cornerstone of embedded systems, allowing the microcontroller to interact with the outside world through simple high and low signals. In this chapter, we've covered the basics of working with GPIO pins—configuring them as inputs and outputs, reading digital signals, and writing to output pins. As you continue through the book, you'll explore more complex I/O operations and learn how to interface with sensors, actuators, and communication protocols.

CHAPTER 6

TIMERS AND COUNTERS

Using Timers to Generate Delays and Time-Based Actions

Timers are essential components in embedded systems, enabling precise control over time-based tasks. A timer is a hardware peripheral inside the microcontroller that counts clock pulses. Timers are commonly used to generate delays, manage periodic tasks, and implement real-time events in embedded applications. They can be used for tasks such as creating time delays, generating PWM signals, or triggering interrupts at regular intervals.

In this section, we will explore how timers work in embedded systems and how you can use them to generate delays and manage time-based actions in C.

1. Basic Concept of Timers

A **timer** is a simple counter that increments or decrements with each clock cycle. It is typically configured to overflow (or reset) after reaching a certain value, which triggers a specific action. Timers can operate in two primary modes:

- **Normal Mode**: The timer counts up from zero to a maximum value (often 255 or 65535) and then overflows back to zero.
- **CTC (Clear Timer on Compare Match) Mode**: In this mode, the timer counts up to a specified value, and when the counter reaches this value, it is cleared (reset to zero), and an interrupt can be triggered.

2. Using Timers for Delays

To generate a time delay, we typically use a timer to count clock cycles and trigger an action once a specific number of cycles have passed. Since the microcontroller's clock operates at a known frequency (e.g., 16 MHz), you can calculate the number of timer ticks required for a specific delay.

Here's a basic example using a timer in an AVR microcontroller to generate a delay:

```c
#include <avr/io.h>
#include <util/delay.h>

#define LED_PIN 0  // Assume the LED is connected
to pin 0 of PORTB
```

```
void init_timer() {
    // Set Timer0 to normal mode
    TCCR0A = 0;     // Clear control register A
    TCCR0B = (1 << CS00);  // Set clock source
(no prescaling, 1x clock speed)
    TCNT0 = 0;      // Initialize the timer count
to zero
}

void delay_ms(uint16_t delay) {
    for (uint16_t i = 0; i < delay; i++) {
        TCNT0 = 0;  // Reset the timer count
        while (TCNT0 < 255);  // Wait until the
timer overflows
    }
}

int main() {
    DDRB |= (1 << LED_PIN);  // Set LED_PIN as an
output

    init_timer();  // Initialize timer

    while (1) {
        PORTB |= (1 << LED_PIN);  // Turn on the
LED
        delay_ms(1000);     //  Delay  for  1000
milliseconds (1 second)
```

```
        PORTB &= ~(1 << LED_PIN);   // Turn off
the LED
        delay_ms(1000);     // Delay for 1000
milliseconds (1 second)
    }

    return 0;
}
```

Explanation:

- **TCCR0A and TCCR0B**: These are control registers for Timer0. The settings configure the timer to count up with no prescaling (the timer counts at the same speed as the microcontroller's clock).
- **TCNT0**: This is the timer counter register. The value in `TCNT0` increments on each clock pulse.
- **delay_ms**: This function generates a delay by waiting for the timer to overflow. The `while (TCNT0 < 255)` loop waits for the timer to reach its maximum value (255 in this case) before continuing.

By adjusting the prescaler (the clock division factor) or using higher-resolution timers, you can fine-tune the timing for more precise delays.

3. Using Timers for Time-Based Actions

In addition to generating delays, timers can be used to trigger time-based actions, such as triggering interrupts after a specific interval, generating PWM signals, or measuring elapsed time.

For example, you can configure a timer to generate a pulse every 1 millisecond, and in that pulse, you can execute time-critical tasks, such as monitoring sensor data or controlling an actuator.

In AVR microcontrollers, this can be achieved using **Timer Interrupts**. Here's an example of setting up a timer interrupt to trigger an action every 1 millisecond:

c

```
#include <avr/io.h>
#include <avr/interrupt.h>

#define LED_PIN 0

void init_timer_interrupt() {
    // Set Timer0 to CTC mode (Clear Timer on
Compare Match)
    TCCR0A = 0;
```

```
    TCCR0B = (1 << WGM02) | (1 << CS00); // CTC
mode with no prescaling
    OCR0A = 249;  // Set compare match value for
1 ms delay at 16 MHz clock

    // Enable timer interrupt
    TIMSK0 = (1 << OCIE0A);

    // Enable global interrupts
    sei();
}

ISR(TIMER0_COMPA_vect) {
    PORTB ^= (1 << LED_PIN);  // Toggle the LED
state (on/off)
}

int main() {
    DDRB |= (1 << LED_PIN);  // Set LED_PIN as an
output

    init_timer_interrupt();  // Initialize timer
interrupt

    while (1) {
        // Main loop does nothing, LED toggling
happens in interrupt
    }
```

```
    return 0;
}
```

Explanation:

- **TCCR0A and TCCR0B**: Configure Timer0 in CTC mode.
- **OCR0A**: This is the compare match register. When the timer reaches the value in `OCR0A` (249), it resets the timer and triggers an interrupt.
- **TIMSK0**: This register enables the interrupt for Timer0 when the compare match occurs.
- **ISR(TIMER0_COMPA_vect)**: This is the interrupt service routine (ISR) that toggles the LED each time the timer reaches the value set in `OCR0A`.

In this setup, the LED toggles every 1 millisecond, based on the timer interrupt.

How Counters Work in Embedded Systems

Counters are essentially timers that count specific events, such as clock pulses, external signals, or input events. They are used in embedded systems to track the number of occurrences of an event, measure time intervals, or generate periodic signals.

A **counter** can be a hardware peripheral inside the microcontroller or a software-based solution that uses an internal timer. Counters can operate in different modes, depending on the event being counted:

1. **Event Counting**: A counter can increment each time a specific event occurs, such as a pulse from a sensor or an external interrupt. For example, you might use a counter to count the number of times a button is pressed within a given time frame.
2. **Time Measurement**: Counters can also be used to measure the time between events. By knowing the clock frequency and the rate at which the counter increments, you can measure time intervals accurately.
3. **PWM Generation**: Counters are often used to generate PWM (Pulse Width Modulation) signals, which are essential for controlling the brightness of LEDs, the speed of motors, or the position of servos.

Example: Simple Event Counting

Here's an example of how to use a counter to count the number of button presses within a fixed period:

c

```
#include <avr/io.h>
#include <avr/interrupt.h>

#define BUTTON_PIN 1

volatile uint16_t button_press_count = 0;

void init_timer_for_counting() {
    // Set Timer1 to normal mode with no prescaling
    TCCR1A = 0;
    TCCR1B = (1 << CS10); // No prescaling (counts at the same speed as system clock)

    // Enable timer overflow interrupt
    TIMSK1 = (1 << TOIE1);

    // Enable global interrupts
    sei();
}

void init_button() {
    // Configure BUTTON_PIN as input
    DDRB &= ~(1 << BUTTON_PIN);
    // Enable pull-up resistor on BUTTON_PIN
    PORTB |= (1 << BUTTON_PIN);
}
```

```
ISR(TIMER1_OVF_vect) {
    // Timer overflow interrupt: Check if the
button is pressed
    if (!(PINB & (1 << BUTTON_PIN))) {
        button_press_count++;    //    Increment
counter on button press
    }
}

int main() {
    init_timer_for_counting();    // Initialize
timer for counting
    init_button();  // Initialize button input

    while (1) {
        // Main loop does nothing, counting
happens in interrupt
        // The count of button presses is stored
in button_press_count
    }

    return 0;
}
```

Explanation:

- **TIMSK1**: Enables the overflow interrupt for Timer1.
- **TIMER1_OVF_vect**: This ISR is triggered when Timer1 overflows. Inside this interrupt, we check the state of the button and increment the count if the button is pressed.

- **button_press_count**: This variable holds the number of button presses detected during the timer's operation.

Conclusion

Timers and counters are indispensable tools in embedded systems for managing time-based actions and events. In this chapter, we've covered how to use timers to generate delays, trigger interrupts, and perform time-critical tasks. We've also explored counters, which are used to track events, measure time, and generate PWM signals. Mastering the use of timers and counters will help you build more sophisticated, real-time embedded applications.

CHAPTER 7

INTERRUPTS IN EMBEDDED SYSTEMS

What Are Interrupts and How to Handle Them?

An **interrupt** is a mechanism that allows the microcontroller to temporarily halt the execution of the main program and switch to an interrupt service routine (ISR) to handle a specific event. Once the interrupt has been serviced, the microcontroller returns to the point in the program where it left off. Interrupts are a crucial part of embedded systems, as they enable real-time responsiveness to external events without continuously polling for them.

In simple terms, an interrupt allows the microcontroller to **react to specific events** (e.g., button presses, sensor readings, or external signals) without wasting processor time constantly checking for those events. Instead of the microcontroller continuously checking if an event has occurred (which would waste CPU cycles), an interrupt "interrupts" the normal program flow and triggers an ISR to handle the event.

1. How Interrupts Work

When an interrupt occurs, the microcontroller:

1. **Pauses the current program execution**: The current instruction is completed, and the program's execution is paused.
2. **Saves the current context**: The microcontroller saves the state of registers, the program counter, and any relevant data that the ISR may need to use. This ensures the program can resume after the interrupt is serviced.
3. **Calls the Interrupt Service Routine (ISR)**: The microcontroller jumps to a predefined location in memory where the ISR is located. The ISR handles the interrupt, such as processing data or reacting to an event.
4. **Restores the context and resumes the program**: Once the ISR has completed its task, the microcontroller restores the saved context and resumes the main program where it was interrupted.

2. Types of Interrupts

Interrupts can be categorized into two types:

- **External Interrupts**: These are caused by external events, such as a button press, a sensor signal, or a signal from another microcontroller. They are typically triggered by specific pins (e.g., GPIO pins) on the microcontroller.

- **Internal Interrupts**: These are triggered by internal events, such as a timer overflow, a UART transmission complete, or a change in an input signal.

3. Why Interrupts Are Useful

Interrupts are essential in embedded systems for several reasons:

- **Real-time responsiveness**: Interrupts enable the system to respond immediately to an event without waiting for the next polling cycle.
- **Efficient resource usage**: The system only reacts to the event when it occurs, saving processing power compared to constantly polling.
- **Handling multiple tasks**: Interrupts allow for concurrent execution of tasks (like handling a sensor reading while maintaining communication).

Setting Up and Managing Interrupts in C

Interrupts must be explicitly enabled and configured in the microcontroller. This often involves setting certain control registers, defining an ISR, and ensuring the interrupt is triggered by the appropriate event. Let's break down how to set up and manage interrupts in C.

1. Enable Global Interrupts

Before enabling specific interrupts, you must globally enable interrupts in the microcontroller. This is typically done by setting a special bit in the global interrupt enable register.

For example, in an AVR microcontroller, you use the `sei()` function to globally enable interrupts:

```c
sei();  // Enable global interrupts
```

Similarly, to disable interrupts, you can use `cli()`:

```c
cli();  // Disable global interrupts
```

2. Setting Up a Timer Interrupt

Let's take an example where we set up an interrupt triggered by a timer overflow. This means that every time the timer overflows (after counting to a maximum value), an interrupt is triggered.

In AVR-based microcontrollers, you typically do the following:

1. **Configure the Timer**: Set the timer to overflow after a certain period.
2. **Enable the Timer Interrupt**: Enable the interrupt flag that corresponds to the timer overflow.
3. **Write the ISR**: Define the ISR to handle the timer interrupt.

Here's an example of how to set up a timer interrupt in an AVR microcontroller using the **Timer0** overflow interrupt:

```c
#include <avr/io.h>
#include <avr/interrupt.h>
#include <util/delay.h>

#define LED_PIN 0  // Assume the LED is connected
to pin 0 of PORTB

void init_timer() {
    // Set Timer0 to normal mode (no prescaling)
    TCCR0A = 0;
    TCCR0B = (1 << CS00);  // No prescaling (use
system clock directly)
```

```
    // Enable Timer0 overflow interrupt
    TIMSK0 = (1 << TOIE0);

    // Enable global interrupts
    sei();
}

ISR(TIMER0_OVF_vect) {
    //  Interrupt  service  routine  for  Timer0
overflow
    PORTB ^= (1 << LED_PIN);  // Toggle the LED
state
}

int main() {
    DDRB |= (1 << LED_PIN);  // Set LED_PIN as an
output

    init_timer();  // Initialize the timer

    while (1) {
        // Main loop does nothing, LED toggling
happens in interrupt
    }

    return 0;
}
```

Explanation:

- **TCCR0A and TCCR0B**: These registers configure Timer0 to operate in normal mode, where the timer counts up without any special behavior.
- **TIMSK0**: This register enables the interrupt for Timer0 overflow.
- **ISR(TIMER0_OVF_vect)**: This is the interrupt service routine for the Timer0 overflow interrupt. When the timer overflows, this ISR is executed, and it toggles the LED state.
- **sei()**: This function enables global interrupts, allowing the microcontroller to respond to interrupts.

3. Setting Up External Interrupts

External interrupts are triggered by events such as a button press or a signal from another device. In most microcontrollers, you configure the external interrupt pins (e.g., INT0, INT1) and specify the event that triggers the interrupt (e.g., rising edge, falling edge, or low level).

Here's an example using an external interrupt to detect a button press:

c

```
#include <avr/io.h>
#include <avr/interrupt.h>

#define BUTTON_PIN 2  // Assume the button is
connected to pin 2 (INT0)

void init_external_interrupt() {
    // Configure INT0 (external interrupt on pin
2) to trigger on a rising edge
    EICRA = (1 << ISC00) | (1 << ISC01);  //
Rising edge triggers the interrupt

    // Enable external interrupt INT0
    EIMSK = (1 << INT0);

    // Enable global interrupts
    sei();
}

ISR(INT0_vect) {
    // Interrupt service routine for external
interrupt INT0
    PORTB ^= (1 << LED_PIN);  // Toggle the LED
state when button is pressed
}

int main() {
    DDRB |= (1 << LED_PIN);  // Set LED_PIN as an
output
```

```
    DDRD &= ~(1 << BUTTON_PIN);     // Set
BUTTON_PIN as an input

    init_external_interrupt();   // Initialize
the external interrupt

    while (1) {
        // Main loop does nothing, LED toggling
happens in interrupt
    }

    return 0;
}
```

Explanation:

- **EICRA**: Configures the external interrupt control register for INT0 to trigger on a rising edge (button press).
- **EIMSK**: Enables the external interrupt for INT0.
- **ISR(INT0_vect)**: This is the interrupt service routine that toggles the LED whenever the button is pressed.

Key Considerations When Using Interrupts

1. **ISR (Interrupt Service Routine)**: Always keep the ISRs as short and efficient as possible. If the ISR takes too long to execute, it could cause missed interrupts or system lag.

2. **Interrupt Priority**: Some microcontrollers allow for interrupt priority settings. Ensure that higher-priority interrupts are serviced first.
3. **Debouncing**: For external interrupts like button presses, ensure that the signal is debounced, either in hardware or software, to avoid false triggers.
4. **Interrupt Flags**: Ensure that interrupt flags are cleared properly after an interrupt is serviced. Otherwise, the interrupt may trigger repeatedly.

Conclusion

Interrupts are an essential feature in embedded systems, allowing the microcontroller to respond to events in real time. In this chapter, we explored how interrupts work, how to handle them, and how to set up and manage interrupts in C. We looked at both **timer interrupts** and **external interrupts**, with practical examples on how to toggle an LED or respond to a button press. Mastering interrupts allows you to create more efficient and responsive embedded systems that can handle multiple tasks simultaneously.

CHAPTER 8

ANALOG-TO-DIGITAL AND DIGITAL-TO-ANALOG CONVERSION

ADC and DAC Fundamentals

In embedded systems, the interaction between the digital world (represented by microcontrollers) and the analog world (represented by real-world signals) is often necessary. Analog signals, such as temperature readings, audio signals, or sensor outputs, are continuous and vary over time, while microcontrollers work with discrete digital signals (0s and 1s). To bridge this gap, we use **Analog-to-Digital Converters (ADC)** and **Digital-to-Analog Converters (DAC)**.

1. Analog-to-Digital Conversion (ADC)

An **ADC** is a device that converts an analog voltage (a continuous signal) into a digital representation that can be processed by a microcontroller. The ADC samples the analog signal at specific intervals and assigns a binary value to each sample based on its amplitude.

Key Concepts in ADC:

- **Resolution**: The resolution of an ADC refers to how finely it can represent the analog signal. It is typically expressed as the number of bits. A higher resolution provides a more accurate digital representation of the analog input.
    - For example, an 8-bit ADC can represent the input with 256 different values (2^8), whereas a 10-bit ADC can represent it with 1024 values (2^10).
- **Sampling Rate**: The sampling rate defines how frequently the ADC samples the analog input. This is crucial for capturing fast-changing signals accurately. For example, in audio applications, the ADC should sample at a rate higher than the frequency of the audio signal to avoid aliasing.
- **Reference Voltage (V_ref)**: The reference voltage defines the maximum voltage that the ADC can measure. The analog input voltage is mapped to a range between 0 and V_ref. If the input voltage exceeds the reference voltage, the ADC will saturate (i.e., it will output the maximum possible value).

2. Digital-to-Analog Conversion (DAC)

A **DAC** does the opposite of an ADC: it converts a digital value (a binary number) into an analog voltage. This allows digital systems to control analog devices, such as motors, speakers, or actuators.

Key Concepts in DAC:

- **Resolution**: Similar to an ADC, a DAC has resolution, typically expressed in bits. A higher-resolution DAC can produce more finely controlled output voltages. An 8-bit DAC can output 256 discrete voltages, while a 12-bit DAC can output 4096 discrete voltages.
- **Output Range**: The DAC has an output range typically determined by a reference voltage. The digital value is mapped to a voltage between 0 and the reference voltage.

Practical Applications of ADC and DAC in Embedded Systems

Both ADCs and DACs are widely used in embedded systems for a variety of applications. Let's look at some common practical uses:

1. Sensor Interfacing with ADC

One of the most common uses of ADCs is for interfacing with sensors that produce analog signals, such as temperature, light, or pressure sensors. Since most microcontrollers work with digital signals, an ADC is used to convert the analog sensor output into a digital value that the microcontroller can process.

Example: Reading Temperature from a Thermistor (ADC)

Thermistors are temperature sensors whose resistance changes with temperature. By using an ADC, we can convert the analog signal from the thermistor into a digital value that can be processed to determine the temperature.

c

```
#include <avr/io.h>
#include <util/delay.h>

#define TEMP_SENSOR_PIN 0    // Assume the thermistor is connected to ADC channel 0

void init_adc() {
```

```
    // Configure ADC to use V_ref as the
reference voltage and right adjust result
    ADMUX = (1 << REFS0);    // Use AVCC as
reference voltage (external 5V or 3.3V)
    ADCSRA = (1 << ADPS2) | (1 << ADPS1) | (1 <<
ADPS0);  // Set prescaler to 16
    ADCSRA |= (1 << ADEN);  // Enable ADC
}

uint16_t read_adc(uint8_t channel) {
    ADMUX = (ADMUX & 0xF0) | (channel & 0x0F);
// Select channel
    ADCSRA |= (1 << ADSC);  // Start conversion
    while (ADCSRA & (1 << ADSC));   // Wait for
conversion to complete
    return ADC;  // Return the 10-bit ADC result
}

int main() {
    init_adc();  // Initialize the ADC

    while (1) {
        uint16_t          adc_result          =
read_adc(TEMP_SENSOR_PIN);   // Read ADC result
from thermistor
        // Convert adc_result to a temperature
value (e.g., using a look-up table or formula)
        _delay_ms(1000);   // Wait for 1 second
before reading again
```

```
    }

    return 0;
}
```

Explanation:

- **ADMUX**: This register selects the ADC input channel (in this case, channel 0).
- **ADCSRA**: This register controls the ADC's operation, including enabling the ADC and starting the conversion.
- **ADC**: The ADC register holds the result of the conversion (a 10-bit value).

In this example, the ADC reads the output of the thermistor, and the microcontroller can then process the digital value to calculate the temperature.

2. Generating Analog Control Signals with DAC

In some applications, the microcontroller needs to generate an analog output signal. This is where DACs come in. For example, a DAC can be used to produce an analog signal to control the brightness of an LED, the speed of a motor, or to output sound in audio applications.

Example: Controlling LED Brightness with PWM and DAC

In this example, the microcontroller uses a DAC to generate a varying voltage that controls the brightness of an LED. The DAC is controlled by a digital value, which could be determined based on user input or sensor data.

```
c

#include <avr/io.h>

#define DAC_PIN 0  // Assume the DAC is connected
to an output pin

void init_dac() {
    // DAC initialization code, depending on the
specific microcontroller and DAC module
}

void set_dac_output(uint16_t value) {
    // Set the DAC output based on the value
(range depends on DAC resolution)
    // Assume the DAC is 8-bit for simplicity
    DAC_OUTPUT_REGISTER = value & 0xFF;  // Only
the lower 8 bits are used
}

int main() {
    init_dac();  // Initialize the DAC
```

```
    uint16_t brightness = 0;    // Start with
lowest brightness

    while (1) {
        set_dac_output(brightness);   // Set the
DAC output to control LED brightness
        brightness = (brightness + 1) % 256;   //
Increase brightness (loop back after 255)
        _delay_ms(10);  // Delay to slow down the
brightness change
    }

    return 0;
}
```

Explanation:

- **DAC_OUTPUT_REGISTER**: This is a placeholder for the DAC's output register where the digital value is written to produce an analog voltage.
- **set_dac_output**: This function sets the DAC's output value, controlling the LED's brightness by varying the output voltage.
- **brightness**: The `brightness` variable controls the LED brightness. It is incremented to increase the output voltage to the DAC.

3. Audio Output with DAC

A common application of DACs in embedded systems is audio output. For example, an embedded system may use a DAC to generate audio signals that drive speakers. The digital audio data can be generated or stored in memory, and the DAC converts it into an analog signal that can be sent to the speaker.

In more complex applications, such as digital synthesizers, DACs are used to produce continuous waveforms (e.g., sine, square, triangle waves) that form the audio signal.

4. Signal Generation and Smoothing

DACs are also commonly used for generating smooth, continuous output signals. For example, in motor control applications, a microcontroller might use a DAC to generate a smooth control voltage for controlling the speed of a motor.

Conclusion

ADCs and DACs play essential roles in connecting embedded systems with the real world. ADCs enable microcontrollers to read real-world analog signals from sensors, while DACs allow microcontrollers to control analog devices. In this chapter, we've covered the fundamentals of ADC and DAC, along with practical applications like reading sensor data, controlling LED brightness, and generating audio signals. Understanding how to use these converters effectively is crucial for creating embedded systems that interact with the physical world.

CHAPTER 9

COMMUNICATION PROTOCOLS: UART

Introduction to UART (Universal Asynchronous Receiver-Transmitter)

UART (Universal Asynchronous Receiver-Transmitter) is one of the most common serial communication protocols used in embedded systems. It allows microcontrollers to communicate with each other and with other devices, such as sensors, modules, or computers, using simple serial data transmission.

UART is **asynchronous**, meaning that there is no clock signal involved between the transmitting and receiving devices. Instead, data is transmitted as a series of bits, with each bit sent at a specific time interval, and the devices must agree on the data rate and other settings.

In UART communication, there are typically two main lines:

1. **TX (Transmit)**: The line used for transmitting data.
2. **RX (Receive)**: The line used for receiving data.

UART communication is full-duplex, meaning data can be sent and received simultaneously, but it requires only two wires for communication, making it simple and efficient for short-distance communication.

Key Concepts in UART Communication

1. **Baud Rate**: The baud rate determines how fast the data is transmitted. It is the number of bits transmitted per second. Common baud rates include 9600, 115200, and 57600 bps (bits per second). Both the transmitter and receiver must operate at the same baud rate for successful communication.
2. **Data Bits**: Typically, data is transmitted in 8-bit chunks, but UART can support configurations with 5, 6, 7, or 9 data bits.
3. **Parity Bit**: The parity bit is an optional error-checking bit that can be added to the data stream. It helps detect errors during transmission. Common parity settings are:
   - **None**: No parity bit.
   - **Even**: Ensures that the number of 1s in the data is even.
   - **Odd**: Ensures that the number of 1s in the data is odd.

4. **Stop Bits**: These bits indicate the end of a data packet. The number of stop bits is typically set to 1, 1.5, or 2, and it allows the receiver to know when a byte has been fully received.
5. **Flow Control**: Some UART systems use flow control to manage the flow of data between the devices. This can be hardware-based (using additional lines like RTS/CTS) or software-based (using XON/XOFF control characters).

Implementing UART Communication in C

To implement UART communication, the microcontroller must be configured to use its UART peripheral. This involves setting the baud rate, data bits, stop bits, and optional parity. After configuration, data can be transmitted or received using the UART's transmit and receive registers.

Let's walk through a basic example of how to set up and use UART for communication in C. For simplicity, this example assumes you are using an AVR microcontroller (e.g., ATmega328p) with the USART (Universal Synchronous and Asynchronous serial Receiver and Transmitter) peripheral.

1. Setting Up UART in C

The steps to configure the UART for communication typically include:

- Setting the baud rate.
- Configuring the frame format (data bits, parity, stop bits).
- Enabling the transmitter and receiver.

Here's a basic code example to configure UART and send data:

```
c

#include <avr/io.h>

#define F_CPU 16000000UL  // Define clock speed
as 16 MHz
#define BAUD 9600            // Desired baud rate
#define MY_UBRR F_CPU/16/BAUD-1  // Calculate the
UBRR value

// Function to initialize UART
void uart_init() {
    unsigned int ubrr = MY_UBRR;
    UBRR0H = (unsigned char)(ubrr >> 8);  // Set
baud rate high byte
    UBRR0L = (unsigned char)(ubrr);        // Set
baud rate low byte
```

```
    UCSR0B = (1 << RXEN0) | (1 << TXEN0); //
Enable receiver and transmitter
    UCSR0C = (1 << UCSZ01) | (1 << UCSZ00); //
Set frame format: 8 data bits, no parity, 1 stop
bit
}

// Function to transmit data via UART
void uart_transmit(unsigned char data) {
    while (!(UCSR0A & (1 << UDRE0))); // Wait for
the transmit buffer to be empty
    UDR0 = data;  // Send the data
}

// Function to receive data via UART
unsigned char uart_receive(void) {
    while (!(UCSR0A & (1 << RXC0)));  // Wait for
data to be received
    return UDR0;  // Get and return received data
from the buffer
}

int main(void) {
    uart_init();  // Initialize UART

    while (1) {
        uart_transmit('A');   // Send character
'A'
        _delay_ms(1000);     // Wait for 1 second
```

```
    }

    return 0;
}
```

Explanation:

- **UBRR**: This register determines the baud rate. The formula `MY_UBRR = F_CPU / 16 / BAUD - 1` is used to calculate the value to load into `UBRR0H` and `UBRR0L`.
- **UCSR0B**: This register enables the UART transmitter (`TXEN0`) and receiver (`RXEN0`).
- **UCSR0C**: This register configures the data frame format, with `UCSZ01` and `UCSZ00` setting the number of data bits to 8.
- **uart_transmit()**: This function waits for the UART data register to be empty and then writes the data to the register for transmission.
- **uart_receive()**: This function waits until data is available in the UART receive register and then returns the received data.

2. Using UART for Communication

Once the UART is initialized, you can send and receive data. For example, to communicate with a sensor or another microcontroller, you can use the following approach:

- **Sending Data**: Use `uart_transmit()` to send data. This function can send individual characters, or you can modify it to send strings or data packets.
- **Receiving Data**: Use `uart_receive()` to receive data from another device. The function waits until a byte is received and returns it.

Example: Echo Program

The following code demonstrates a simple UART communication program where the microcontroller echoes back received data:

```c
c

#include <avr/io.h>

#define F_CPU 16000000UL
#define BAUD 9600
#define MY_UBRR F_CPU/16/BAUD-1

void uart_init() {
    unsigned int ubrr = MY_UBRR;
    UBRR0H = (unsigned char)(ubrr >> 8);
    UBRR0L = (unsigned char)(ubrr);
    UCSR0B = (1 << RXEN0) | (1 << TXEN0);
    UCSR0C = (1 << UCSZ01) | (1 << UCSZ00);
}
```

```
void uart_transmit(unsigned char data) {
    while (!(UCSR0A & (1 << UDRE0)));
    UDR0 = data;
}

unsigned char uart_receive(void) {
    while (!(UCSR0A & (1 << RXC0)));
    return UDR0;
}

int main(void) {
    uart_init();

    unsigned char received_data;

    while (1) {
        received_data = uart_receive();     //
Receive data
        uart_transmit(received_data);    // Echo
the received data
    }

    return 0;
}
```

3. Advanced UART Features

Some advanced features of UART include:

- **Interrupts**: UART communication can be interrupt-driven. This allows the microcontroller to perform other tasks while waiting for data to be received, instead of constantly polling the UART receiver.
- **Flow Control**: While not always necessary, flow control mechanisms like **RTS/CTS** (Request to Send / Clear to Send) can be implemented to manage the flow of data, especially in cases where data is being transferred at high speeds.
- **Multi-Device Communication**: UART can be used to communicate with multiple devices by connecting the TX and RX pins to a multiplexer or using UART-based communication protocols such as RS-485 or RS-232.

Conclusion

UART is a simple, yet powerful, communication protocol that allows embedded systems to exchange data with other devices. In this chapter, we explored the fundamentals of UART, including baud rates, data bits, stop bits, and parity. We also covered practical examples of setting up UART communication in C, sending and receiving data, and some advanced features like interrupts and flow control.

By understanding and implementing UART communication, you can develop embedded systems that interact with a variety of peripherals, sensors, and other microcontrollers, opening the door to a wide range of applications, from data logging to real-time control systems.

CHAPTER 10

I2C PROTOCOL

Overview of the I2C Protocol

The **I2C (Inter-Integrated Circuit)** protocol is a widely used communication protocol in embedded systems for connecting microcontrollers to peripherals such as sensors, memory, display modules, and more. I2C is a synchronous, **multi-master, multi-slave** communication protocol, meaning it can support multiple devices (both master and slave devices) on a single communication bus.

I2C uses only two wires to communicate:

1. **SDA (Serial Data Line)**: This is the line used to transfer data between devices.
2. **SCL (Serial Clock Line)**: This line carries the clock signal that synchronizes the data transfer.

The devices connected via I2C are assigned unique addresses, and data is sent in a **master-slave** configuration. The master device controls the communication, while the slave devices respond based on the master's requests.

Key Features of I2C:

1. **Two-Wire Interface**: I2C uses only two lines, SDA and SCL, which makes it simpler and more efficient than other communication protocols like SPI, which require more lines.
2. **Multi-Master**: Multiple master devices can exist on the bus, allowing for flexibility in the system design.
3. **Addressing**: Each slave device on the I2C bus has a unique address, typically 7 bits (up to 127 devices), or 10 bits in extended mode.
4. **Bidirectional Data Transfer**: Both the SDA and SCL lines are shared by all devices, and data can be transferred in both directions: from master to slave or vice versa.
5. **Synchronous Communication**: I2C transfers are synchronized to the clock (SCL), and data is valid on the rising edge of the clock.
6. **Speed**: I2C supports multiple speeds, ranging from 100 kbps (Standard Mode) to 400 kbps (Fast Mode), and higher speeds (up to 3.4 Mbps) in High-Speed Mode.

1. Basic I2C Communication Flow

In I2C communication, the master initiates communication by sending a **start condition** (S). The start condition signals that data will follow. The master then sends the 7-bit address of the slave device, followed by a **read** or **write** bit that indicates the operation type. If the operation is a write, the master will send data to the slave, while if the operation is a read, the slave will send data to the master.

The communication ends with a **stop condition** (P), which tells all devices that the communication is complete and they can release the bus.

Typical I2C Data Frame:

- **Start Condition** (S)
- **Slave Address** (7 bits)
- **Read/Write Bit** (1 bit)
- **Data** (8 bits)
- **Acknowledge** (ACK) after each byte
- **Stop Condition** (P)

Interfacing Sensors and Peripherals with I2C in Embedded Systems

I2C is widely used to interface with various sensors, displays, EEPROMs, and other peripherals in embedded systems. In this section, we will go over how to interface an I2C device (e.g., a temperature sensor) with a microcontroller, using C for programming.

1. I2C Bus Architecture

In an I2C bus, there is always one master device, which controls the communication. The master communicates with slave devices by sending their addresses.

- **Master**: Typically a microcontroller, responsible for initiating communication and controlling the bus.
- **Slave**: Any peripheral device (e.g., sensor, EEPROM) that responds to the master's commands.

2. I2C Master Configuration

To communicate with an I2C device, the microcontroller must be configured as an I2C master. Most microcontrollers (e.g., AVR, STM32, PIC) have built-in I2C peripherals, making it easier to set up I2C communication in embedded systems. The configuration involves setting the clock rate (baud rate) for the communication and enabling the I2C peripheral.

3. I2C Data Transfer: Writing to a Slave Device

To write data to a slave device, the master first sends the slave's 7-bit address, followed by a write bit (0). Then, the master can send one or more bytes of data, and the slave acknowledges each byte.

Example: Writing Data to a Slave Device Here is an example of how to send data to a slave device (for instance, a temperature sensor) in C using I2C on an AVR microcontroller:

```
c

#include <avr/io.h>
#include <util/twi.h> // Include for TWI (I2C)
functions

#define SLAVE_ADDRESS 0x48   // Example 7-bit
address of the slave device

void i2c_init() {
    TWSR = 0;                 // Set prescaler to 1
    TWBR = 32;                 // Set SCL frequency
(100kHz if F_CPU = 16 MHz)
    TWCR = (1 << TWEN);     // Enable TWI (I2C)
}

void i2c_start() {
    TWCR = (1 << TWSTA) | (1 << TWINT) | (1 <<
TWEN); // Send START condition
    while (!(TWCR & (1 << TWINT))); // Wait until
the start condition is transmitted
}

void i2c_stop() {
```

```
    TWCR = (1 << TWSTO) | (1 << TWINT) | (1 <<
TWEN); // Send STOP condition
    while (TWCR & (1 << TWSTO)); // Wait for stop
condition to be transmitted
}

void i2c_write(uint8_t data) {
    TWDR = data;                    // Load data into
TWI Data Register
    TWCR = (1 << TWINT) | (1 << TWEN); // Start
the transmission
    while (!(TWCR & (1 << TWINT))); // Wait for
the transmission to complete
}

int main() {
    i2c_init();                //    Initialize    I2C
communication
    i2c_start();   // Send the start condition

    i2c_write(SLAVE_ADDRESS << 1);   // Send the
slave address (write mode)
    i2c_write(0x01);  // Send data (e.g., command
to start temperature reading)

    i2c_stop();   // Send the stop condition

    while (1);    // Infinite loop
```

```
    return 0;
}
```

Explanation:

- **i2c_init()**: Initializes the I2C communication by setting the SCL clock rate and enabling the TWI peripheral.
- **i2c_start()**: Sends a start condition, indicating that communication will begin.
- **i2c_write()**: Sends data byte by byte to the slave device.
- **i2c_stop()**: Sends a stop condition to release the bus.

In this example, we are writing data to a slave device with address `0x48` (a hypothetical temperature sensor). After the slave address, we send the data byte `0x01`, which could be a command to start the temperature reading.

4. I2C Data Transfer: Reading from a Slave Device

To read data from an I2C slave device, the master sends the slave's address (in write mode), followed by a read request (usually sending the address byte, followed by a read bit 1). The master then reads the received data from the I2C bus.

Example: Reading Data from a Slave Device

Here's an example of how to read data from a slave device (e.g., the same temperature sensor):

```c
c

#include <avr/io.h>
#include <util/twi.h>

#define SLAVE_ADDRESS 0x48  // Slave address

uint8_t i2c_read() {
    TWCR = (1 << TWINT) | (1 << TWEN) | (1 << TWEA); // Send the start condition and enable acknowledgment
    while (!(TWCR & (1 << TWINT)));  // Wait for the data to be received
    return TWDR;  // Return the received data
}

void i2c_read_data() {
    i2c_start();  // Send start condition
    i2c_write(SLAVE_ADDRESS << 1);  // Send slave address (write mode)
    i2c_write(0x00);  // Send register address or command to read from

    i2c_start();  // Send repeated start condition
    i2c_write((SLAVE_ADDRESS << 1) | 1);  // Send slave address (read mode)
```

```
    uint8_t data = i2c_read();  // Read data from
slave
    i2c_stop();  // Send stop condition
}

int main() {
    i2c_init();  // Initialize I2C
    i2c_read_data();   // Read data from the
sensor

    while (1);  // Infinite loop

    return 0;
}
```

Explanation:

- **i2c_read()**: This function reads a byte of data from the I2C bus.
- **i2c_read_data()**: This function sends a read command to the slave device, performs a repeated start, and reads the data byte.

5. Practical Applications of I2C in Embedded Systems

1. **Sensor Interfacing**: Many sensors, such as temperature sensors, pressure sensors, accelerometers, and gyroscopes, communicate via I2C. These sensors usually have a small, unique

address, making them easy to integrate into systems with multiple devices.

2. **EEPROM and Flash Memory**: I2C is often used to interface with external memory modules like EEPROMs and Flash memory. These non-volatile memories are used for storing configurations or data logging.
3. **Display Modules**: I2C is used to control display modules like OLED screens and character LCDs. By sending commands and data via I2C, the microcontroller can display information on these devices.
4. **Real-Time Clocks (RTC)**: Many RTC modules use I2C to communicate with microcontrollers to provide timekeeping functionality.
5. **Expanding I/O**: I2C is also used to expand I/O capabilities in systems, where a master microcontroller can communicate with multiple I/O expanders like the PCF8574 to increase the number of available GPIO pins.

Conclusion

The I2C protocol is a versatile, simple, and widely used communication protocol in embedded systems, enabling easy and efficient communication between microcontrollers and peripherals. In this chapter, we explored the fundamentals of I2C communication, including how it works, addressing, and the process of sending and receiving data. We also looked at practical examples of interfacing I2C-based sensors and peripherals with microcontrollers. By understanding and utilizing I2C, you can create powerful and flexible embedded systems capable of communicating with a wide range of devices.

CHAPTER 11

SPI PROTOCOL

Introduction to the Serial Peripheral Interface (SPI)

SPI (Serial Peripheral Interface) is a synchronous serial communication protocol commonly used in embedded systems to exchange data between a master device (typically a microcontroller) and one or more peripheral devices (e.g., sensors, memory chips, displays, or other microcontrollers). Unlike I2C, which is a multi-master protocol, SPI is a full-duplex communication protocol where the master device controls the communication and usually has a dedicated connection with each peripheral.

SPI uses four lines for communication:

1. **MOSI (Master Out, Slave In)**: This line carries data from the master device to the slave device.
2. **MISO (Master In, Slave Out)**: This line carries data from the slave device to the master device.
3. **SCK (Serial Clock)**: This clock signal is generated by the master device and synchronizes the data transmission between the master and the slave.

4. **SS (Slave Select)**: This line is used to select the active slave device in multi-slave setups. When the SS pin is low, the slave is selected and ready to communicate.

Key Features of SPI:

1. **Full-Duplex**: Data can be sent and received simultaneously.
2. **Clock Synchronization**: SPI communication is synchronized using a clock signal generated by the master device.
3. **High Speed**: SPI can achieve high data rates compared to other protocols like I2C, making it suitable for high-speed applications.
4. **Simple Protocol**: SPI is relatively simple to implement and requires fewer wires compared to other serial protocols like UART.

SPI Communication Sequence:

1. The master device sends a clock signal (SCK) to the slave.
2. The master sends data via the MOSI line, and the slave simultaneously sends data back to the master via the MISO line.
3. The master selects which slave to communicate with by pulling the corresponding **SS** (Slave Select) pin low.

4. Data is transferred in chunks (usually 8 bits), and both devices acknowledge receipt at each clock cycle.

Writing Code to Communicate with SPI Devices

To use SPI in an embedded system, the master device needs to be configured to control the SPI peripheral. This configuration involves setting the clock polarity, clock phase, and the data order (MSB or LSB first). Let's go through a basic example of how to communicate with an SPI device, such as a sensor or memory chip, using a microcontroller (e.g., AVR microcontroller like ATmega328p).

1. Setting Up SPI on the Master Device

In this example, we'll set up the SPI peripheral on an AVR microcontroller to send and receive data from an SPI slave device.

Steps to Configure SPI:

- Set the **SPI mode**: The SPI mode determines the clock polarity (CPOL) and clock phase (CPHA). For AVR, we will use Mode 0 (CPOL = 0, CPHA = 0), where the clock is low when idle, and data is sampled on the rising edge of the clock.

- Set the **data order**: The order of transmission of the data can be **MSB (Most Significant Bit) first** or **LSB (Least Significant Bit) first**. We'll use MSB first.
- Set the **clock rate**: This determines the speed of the SPI communication. The clock speed is divided by a prescaler value.

2. SPI Master Setup in C

Here is an example of configuring the SPI peripheral on an AVR microcontroller (ATmega328p) to communicate with an SPI slave device:

```
c

#include <avr/io.h>

#define SS_PIN 4    // Slave Select pin on PORTB
#define MOSI_PIN 5 // Master Out Slave In (MOSI)
pin on PORTB
#define MISO_PIN 6 // Master In Slave Out (MISO)
pin on PORTB
#define SCK_PIN 7   // Serial Clock (SCK) pin on
PORTB

// Function to initialize SPI as Master
void spi_init_master() {
```

```
    // Set MOSI, SCK, and SS as output, MISO as input
    DDRB = (1 << MOSI_PIN) | (1 << SCK_PIN) | (1 << SS_PIN);
    DDRB &= ~(1 << MISO_PIN);   // Set MISO as input

    // Enable SPI, set as master, set clock rate (F_CPU / 16)
    SPCR = (1 << SPE) | (1 << MSTR) | (1 << SPR0);
}

// Function to send and receive a byte via SPI
uint8_t spi_transmit(uint8_t data) {
    SPDR = data;  // Load data into the SPI data register
    while (!(SPSR & (1 << SPIF)));  // Wait for the transmission to complete
    return SPDR;  // Return received data from SPI Data Register
}

// Function to select the slave device
void select_slave() {
    PORTB &= ~(1 << SS_PIN);  // Pull SS pin low to select the slave
}

// Function to deselect the slave device
```

```
void deselect_slave() {
    PORTB |= (1 << SS_PIN);  // Pull SS pin high
to deselect the slave
}

int main(void) {
    uint8_t received_data;

    // Initialize SPI as master
    spi_init_master();

    while (1) {
        select_slave();    // Select the slave
device
        received_data = spi_transmit(0x55);   //
Send a data byte and receive the response
        deselect_slave();  // Deselect the slave
device

        // Do something with the received data
(e.g., store, process, or display it)
    }

    return 0;
}
```

Explanation:

1. **spi_init_master()**: This function sets up the microcontroller's SPI peripheral in master mode. The

necessary pins (MOSI, SCK, SS) are set as outputs, while the MISO pin is set as an input.

  - **SPCR**: The SPI Control Register is configured to enable SPI, set the microcontroller as the master, and set the clock rate.

2. **spi_transmit()**: This function sends a byte of data via SPI and waits for the reception of a byte in return. It sends the byte via the **SPDR** (SPI Data Register) and waits for the SPI Interrupt Flag (SPIF) to indicate that the transmission is complete.
3. **select_slave()**: This function pulls the **SS** pin low, which selects the slave device for communication.
4. **deselect_slave()**: This function pulls the **SS** pin high, which deselects the slave device and terminates the communication.

3. Communication with a SPI Slave Device

In the example above, the microcontroller sends a byte (`0x55`) to the SPI slave device and receives a byte in return. The process is as follows:

- **Master sends data**: The master (microcontroller) sends a data byte via the **MOSI** line.
- **Slave responds**: The slave device receives the data on its **MOSI** pin and may respond with data on the **MISO** line.

- **Master receives data**: The master receives the response on the **MISO** line.

This basic example demonstrates sending and receiving a byte of data in SPI mode.

4. SPI Clock Speed and Timing

The clock speed in SPI communication is typically set by dividing the system clock by a prescaler value. In the example, we set the prescaler to divide the clock by 16, which means the clock frequency of the SPI bus will be **F_CPU / 16**. For example, if the system clock is 16 MHz, the SPI clock will run at 1 MHz.

You can modify the SPI clock speed by adjusting the **SPR0** and **SPR1** bits in the **SPCR** register, or by setting the appropriate prescaler value in the **SPSR** register.

5. Multi-Slave SPI Configuration

In a multi-slave SPI setup, the master communicates with multiple slaves by selecting and deselecting them via the **SS** (Slave Select) line. Each slave device has its own **SS** pin, and the master pulls the corresponding **SS** pin low to initiate communication with the desired slave. After the communication is complete, the **SS** pin is pulled high to deselect the slave.

Conclusion

The **SPI protocol** is an efficient, high-speed communication method widely used in embedded systems for interfacing with peripherals. In this chapter, we covered the basics of the SPI protocol, how to set up SPI communication in C on a microcontroller, and how to communicate with SPI slave devices. SPI is especially useful when you need high-speed communication, and by understanding its implementation, you can easily interface with a variety of peripherals, such as sensors, memory devices, and display modules.

CHAPTER 12

REAL-TIME OPERATING SYSTEMS (RTOS) OVERVIEW

What is an RTOS and How It Differs from Regular Operating Systems?

A **Real-Time Operating System (RTOS)** is an operating system designed to manage hardware resources and execute tasks in a predictable, timely manner. Unlike regular operating systems (e.g., Linux, Windows), which focus on maximizing throughput and overall system efficiency, an RTOS is optimized for meeting time-critical deadlines and ensuring that tasks are completed within a specified time frame.

In embedded systems, real-time constraints are often crucial. For example, in a medical device, the system must respond to sensor data and trigger alerts in real time, without delay. An RTOS guarantees that high-priority tasks, such as reading sensor data or controlling actuators, get immediate attention when needed.

Key Differences Between RTOS and Regular Operating Systems:

1. **Task Scheduling**:
   - **RTOS**: An RTOS uses deterministic scheduling, where tasks are executed at precisely the right time, according to their priority or deadlines. This guarantees that time-critical tasks are always executed within a defined time frame.
   - **Regular OS**: A regular operating system, such as Linux, uses general-purpose scheduling to maximize overall throughput, often without strict guarantees for when specific tasks will be executed.
2. **Task Prioritization**:
   - **RTOS**: Tasks in an RTOS are typically assigned priorities. Higher-priority tasks preempt lower-priority ones to meet real-time deadlines.
   - **Regular OS**: While modern operating systems can support priority-based task scheduling, they generally aim to balance all tasks and may not always prioritize time-critical tasks over others.
3. **Preemption**:
   - **RTOS**: An RTOS allows **preemptive scheduling**, where a higher-priority task can preempt (interrupt) a lower-priority task at any time.

   - **Regular OS**: In non-real-time operating systems, task preemption occurs, but it's more geared towards ensuring fairness and load balancing rather than meeting real-time deadlines.

4. **Predictability and Reliability**:
   - **RTOS**: An RTOS is designed to provide **predictability**, ensuring tasks will meet deadlines with minimal jitter (variability in response time). It guarantees that critical operations are executed reliably and on time.
   - **Regular OS**: While modern operating systems provide reasonable performance and can be optimized for responsiveness, they cannot guarantee strict timing constraints required for time-sensitive applications.
5. **Resource Management**:
   - **RTOS**: An RTOS carefully manages resources (e.g., CPU, memory) to ensure that tasks execute within their time constraints. It often includes features like priority-based scheduling, inter-task communication, and real-time synchronization mechanisms.
   - **Regular OS**: Regular operating systems are optimized for general-purpose computing and multitasking, without strict resource management for time-sensitive tasks.

6. **Determinism**:
   - **RTOS**: An RTOS is **deterministic**, meaning that the system behavior is predictable and that tasks execute within specified time limits.
   - **Regular OS**: A regular operating system is not deterministic and may exhibit variable latency and unpredictable task execution times.

Key Components of an RTOS:

1. **Task Management**: The RTOS handles task scheduling and execution. It allows tasks to be prioritized, preempted, and managed based on their timing requirements.
2. **Inter-Task Communication**: RTOSes provide mechanisms like **semaphores**, **message queues**, and **mailboxes** for tasks to communicate with each other and synchronize their operations.
3. **Memory Management**: RTOSes have optimized memory management, allowing tasks to efficiently use memory while avoiding memory fragmentation.
4. **Timers and Clocks**: Real-time tasks are usually time-triggered, and the RTOS includes support for precise timers and clock management to ensure tasks run at the right time.

5. **Interrupt Management**: An RTOS typically supports interrupt handling with low latency, ensuring immediate response to hardware events.

Setting Up a Basic RTOS Environment for Embedded Systems

In this section, we'll go through the steps to set up a basic RTOS environment on an embedded system. We'll focus on using a popular RTOS, such as **FreeRTOS**, which is widely used in embedded applications due to its simplicity, open-source nature, and broad platform support.

1. Choosing an RTOS

While FreeRTOS is one of the most popular choices, other RTOS options include **ChibiOS**, **RTEMS**, and **Micrium OS**. When choosing an RTOS for your embedded system, consider factors such as:

- **CPU architecture support** (ARM, AVR, etc.)
- **Real-time constraints**
- **Memory footprint**
- **Task synchronization features**
- **Community and support**

For this example, we'll use FreeRTOS, which is lightweight, highly configurable, and has excellent support for a wide range of microcontrollers.

2. Installing FreeRTOS

To get started with FreeRTOS, you'll need:

- A microcontroller (e.g., STM32, ARM Cortex, or AVR).
- A toolchain (such as GCC) to compile the code.
- An IDE (like STM32CubeIDE or Atmel Studio) or a build system (like Makefiles).

You can download FreeRTOS from its official website (https://www.freertos.org) or from the FreeRTOS GitHub repository (https://github.com/FreeRTOS).

3. Setting Up the FreeRTOS Kernel

After setting up the toolchain and IDE, the next step is to configure the FreeRTOS kernel for your target microcontroller. This involves:

- **Configuring the FreeRTOS tick rate**: The tick rate is the frequency at which the RTOS kernel's scheduler runs. It's typically set to 1 ms, meaning the scheduler will run every 1 ms to check for any tasks that need to be executed.

- **Configuring memory management**: FreeRTOS supports dynamic memory allocation (e.g., using `malloc()` or `pvPortMalloc()`), but you can also configure it to use a static memory model for better predictability in embedded systems.

4. Creating Tasks

In FreeRTOS, tasks are functions that execute independently. Tasks can be configured with specific priorities and stack sizes. Here's an example of how to create tasks in FreeRTOS.

Example: Simple Task Creation in FreeRTOS

```c
c

#include "FreeRTOS.h"
#include "task.h"

// Task function
void vTask1(void *pvParameters) {
    for (;;) {
        // Code to run in Task 1
```

```
        // Toggle an LED or perform some operation
    }
}

void vTask2(void *pvParameters) {
    for (;;) {
        // Code to run in Task 2
        // Read sensor data or perform some operation
    }
}

int main(void) {
    // Create tasks
    xTaskCreate(vTask1, "Task1", 128, NULL, 1, NULL);
    xTaskCreate(vTask2, "Task2", 128, NULL, 1, NULL);

    // Start the scheduler
    vTaskStartScheduler();

    // If all goes well, the program will never reach here
    for (;;) {}
    return 0;
}
```

Explanation:

- **xTaskCreate()**: This function is used to create tasks in FreeRTOS. You specify the task function, name, stack size, parameters, priority, and a handle (optional).
- **vTaskStartScheduler()**: This function starts the FreeRTOS kernel scheduler, which begins task execution according to their priorities and the available time slices.

5. Task Scheduling and Priorities

FreeRTOS uses a priority-based preemptive scheduling algorithm. The tasks with the highest priority will be executed first, and if there's a task of equal priority, the RTOS will use round-robin scheduling to execute them.

When configuring tasks, you can assign priorities based on the criticality of the task. For instance, a real-time sensor reading task would have a higher priority than a periodic status update task.

6. Inter-Task Communication

FreeRTOS provides several mechanisms for tasks to communicate with each other:

- **Queues**: To pass data between tasks safely.

- **Semaphores and Mutexes**: To synchronize tasks and prevent conflicts when accessing shared resources.
- **Event Groups**: To allow tasks to wait for certain events to occur before executing.

Example of using a queue to send data between tasks:

```c
xQueueHandle xQueue;

void vTaskProducer(void *pvParameters) {
    int data = 100;
    for (;;) {
        xQueueSend(xQueue,                    &data,
portMAX_DELAY);
        vTaskDelay(1000  /  portTICK_PERIOD_MS);
// Delay for 1 second
    }
}

void vTaskConsumer(void *pvParameters) {
    int receivedData;
    for (;;) {
        if (xQueueReceive(xQueue, &receivedData,
portMAX_DELAY) == pdPASS) {
            // Process received data
        }
    }
```

```
}

int main(void) {
    // Create the queue with space for 10
integers
    xQueue = xQueueCreate(10, sizeof(int));

    // Create producer and consumer tasks
    xTaskCreate(vTaskProducer, "Producer", 128,
NULL, 1, NULL);
    xTaskCreate(vTaskConsumer, "Consumer", 128,
NULL, 1, NULL);

    // Start the scheduler
    vTaskStartScheduler();

    for (;;) {}
    return 0;
}
```

7. Timers and Interrupts

Timers and interrupts are crucial for real-time systems. FreeRTOS has built-in support for hardware timers, and it allows you to create software timers that execute after a defined period. Interrupts can also trigger tasks or signal events to tasks.

Conclusion

Real-Time Operating Systems (RTOS) are crucial for applications that require deterministic, predictable behavior. They ensure that tasks are completed on time and provide mechanisms for handling time-critical operations in embedded systems. In this chapter, we explored the core concepts of RTOS, how they differ from regular operating systems, and how to set up a basic RTOS environment using FreeRTOS. By leveraging the features of an RTOS, embedded developers can create responsive, reliable, and efficient systems for time-sensitive applications.

CHAPTER 13

TASK MANAGEMENT AND SCHEDULING IN RTOS

Task Management Concepts and How Tasks Are Scheduled in an RTOS

In an embedded system, an RTOS (Real-Time Operating System) plays a crucial role in managing tasks and ensuring that the system meets its timing requirements. Task management in an RTOS refers to the creation, execution, and scheduling of tasks based on their priorities and deadlines.

Task management involves several key concepts:

1. **Tasks**: A **task** (also known as a thread or process) is a unit of work that the RTOS schedules and manages. Tasks can represent various functions, such as sensor reading, motor control, communication handling, and user interface updates. Each task in an RTOS runs independently but shares the system's resources (e.g., CPU, memory).

2. **Task Control Block (TCB)**: The RTOS maintains a **Task Control Block (TCB)** for each task. The TCB stores the task's state, priority, stack pointer, program counter, and other task-related data. It allows the RTOS to manage tasks efficiently by tracking their execution.
3. **Task States**: Tasks in an RTOS can be in different states, such as:
   - **Ready**: The task is ready to be executed, but it is waiting for the CPU.
   - **Running**: The task is currently being executed by the CPU.
   - **Blocked**: The task is waiting for an event or resource (e.g., waiting for a semaphore, or for input data).
   - **Suspended**: The task is temporarily inactive, typically due to system-level controls or external requests.
4. **Task Priorities**: RTOSes often use a **priority-based scheduling** model, where each task is assigned a priority. Tasks with higher priority preempt lower-priority tasks. The RTOS scheduler always attempts to execute the highest-priority task that is ready to run. Priority schemes can be:

- **Fixed priority**: Tasks are assigned fixed priorities that don't change.
- **Dynamic priority**: Priorities change during execution, depending on task behavior or external conditions.

5. **Preemptive vs. Cooperative Scheduling**:
   - **Preemptive scheduling**: In a preemptive RTOS, tasks with higher priority can preempt tasks with lower priority. This means that a running task can be interrupted by a higher-priority task.
   - **Cooperative scheduling**: In a cooperative RTOS, tasks must voluntarily yield control of the CPU. A task cannot be preempted; it must call an API to voluntarily yield control to other tasks.
6. **Context Switching**: **Context switching** is the process by which the RTOS saves the state (context) of a task (such as its CPU registers) and restores the state of another task. This occurs when the RTOS switches between tasks, typically due to an interrupt, task preemption, or voluntary yielding.
7. **Schedulers**: The **scheduler** is responsible for determining which task should run next. It uses the task priorities and states to make this decision. The scheduler can be:

- **Fixed-priority preemptive scheduler**: It assigns tasks priorities statically and preempts lower-priority tasks when higher-priority tasks are ready to run.
- **Round-robin scheduler**: Tasks of equal priority are executed in a circular order, with each task running for a specific time slice.

How Tasks Are Scheduled in an RTOS

1. **Task Creation**: Tasks in an RTOS are created by the **xTaskCreate()** function (in FreeRTOS) or similar functions in other RTOSes. During task creation, you define the task function, priority, stack size, and other parameters. Once created, the task enters the ready state and is eligible to be scheduled by the RTOS.
2. **Task Scheduling**: The RTOS scheduler runs periodically to determine which task should be executed next. The decision is based on:
   - **Task priorities**: The scheduler always selects the highest-priority task that is in the ready state.
   - **Time slices** (in case of tasks with equal priority): The scheduler gives each task a time slice (quantum) to run before switching to the next task.

- **Blocking operations**: A task may be blocked while waiting for an event, resource, or synchronization mechanism, which causes the scheduler to select a different task.

3. **Preemption and Task Switching**: When a higher-priority task becomes ready to run, the RTOS will perform a **context switch**. The current task is suspended, and its context is saved. Then, the higher-priority task's context is loaded, and it begins execution. This ensures that high-priority tasks are executed without delay.
4. **Blocking and Synchronization**: A task can enter a blocked state if it is waiting for an event or resource. The RTOS provides mechanisms like **semaphores**, **message queues**, and **event flags** to synchronize tasks and ensure they can communicate and wait for events.

Implementing Tasks Using RTOS in Embedded Systems

Now that we understand task management and scheduling, let's implement tasks in an RTOS environment using FreeRTOS. FreeRTOS is widely used for embedded applications and provides an easy way to manage tasks.

Steps to Create Tasks in FreeRTOS:

1. **Task Function**: Define a task function that contains the code to be executed by the task.
2. **xTaskCreate()**: Use the `xTaskCreate()` function to create tasks. You define the task's function, stack size, priority, and handle.
3. **Task Scheduler**: Once the tasks are created, call `vTaskStartScheduler()` to start the FreeRTOS scheduler, which will begin executing tasks according to their priorities.

Example: Creating Tasks in FreeRTOS

In this example, we will create two tasks: one for blinking an LED and another for reading a sensor.

```
c

#include "FreeRTOS.h"
#include "task.h"
#include <avr/io.h>
#include <util/delay.h>

#define LED_PIN 0
#define SENSOR_PIN 1

// Task for blinking the LED
void vTaskBlinkLED(void *pvParameters) {
```

```
    DDRB |= (1 << LED_PIN);  // Set LED pin as
output
    while (1) {
        PORTB ^= (1 << LED_PIN);  // Toggle the
LED
        vTaskDelay(500 / portTICK_PERIOD_MS);
// Delay for 500ms
    }
}

// Task for reading a sensor
void vTaskReadSensor(void *pvParameters) {
    DDRB &= ~(1 << SENSOR_PIN);  // Set sensor
pin as input
    while (1) {
        if (PINB & (1 << SENSOR_PIN)) {
            // Sensor is high
        } else {
            // Sensor is low
        }
        vTaskDelay(1000 / portTICK_PERIOD_MS);
// Delay for 1 second
    }
}

int main(void) {
    // Create tasks
    xTaskCreate(vTaskBlinkLED, "Blink LED", 128,
NULL, 1, NULL);
```

```
    xTaskCreate(vTaskReadSensor, "Read Sensor", 128, NULL, 1, NULL);

    // Start the scheduler
    vTaskStartScheduler();

    // If all goes well, the program will never reach here
    while (1) {}
    return 0;
}
```

Explanation:

- **vTaskBlinkLED()**: This task blinks an LED every 500 milliseconds. It toggles the LED and then delays for 500 ms using `vTaskDelay()`.
- **vTaskReadSensor()**: This task checks the state of a sensor every second. It reads the sensor pin and processes the result.
- **vTaskCreate()**: We create the two tasks using `xTaskCreate()`. The function takes the task function, task name, stack size, parameters, priority, and a task handle.
- **vTaskStartScheduler()**: Starts the FreeRTOS scheduler, which begins executing the tasks.

Key RTOS Concepts Implemented:

1. **Task Creation**: Using `xTaskCreate()`, we create two tasks, each with its own function, stack size, and priority.
2. **Task Delay**: We use `vTaskDelay()` to add a delay to the tasks, allowing for cooperative multitasking and giving the RTOS scheduler a chance to switch between tasks.
3. **Task Scheduling**: The FreeRTOS scheduler automatically manages task switching based on priorities and delays.

Conclusion

In this chapter, we explored **task management** and **scheduling** in Real-Time Operating Systems (RTOS). We discussed how tasks are managed, their states, and the different types of scheduling used in RTOS. We also covered how to create and manage tasks in embedded systems using FreeRTOS, and we demonstrated how to write simple tasks that interact with hardware peripherals like LEDs and sensors. Understanding task management and scheduling is crucial for building reliable, time-critical embedded systems that meet real-time requirements. By leveraging RTOS features, developers can ensure that tasks execute efficiently and in a timely manner, even in complex embedded systems.

CHAPTER 14

MEMORY MANAGEMENT IN EMBEDDED SYSTEMS

Understanding Memory Types: SRAM, Flash, EEPROM

Memory management is a critical aspect of embedded system design because embedded devices often have limited memory resources. Efficient use of available memory is crucial for ensuring that the system functions properly without running out of memory or causing errors. There are several types of memory commonly used in embedded systems, each with distinct characteristics and uses.

1. SRAM (Static Random-Access Memory)

SRAM is a type of volatile memory used for temporary data storage. It is faster than other types of memory like DRAM and retains data as long as power is supplied. However, once power is lost, the data stored in SRAM is lost.

Key Characteristics of SRAM:

- **Volatile**: SRAM loses its data when power is turned off.

- **Fast Access**: It provides faster access times compared to other types of memory like DRAM.
- **Used for**: Storing variables, data buffers, and stack information during program execution.

Applications of SRAM:

- **Temporary storage** for data that needs to be quickly accessed, such as variables during program execution or real-time data buffers.
- **Stack memory**: Used for function calls, local variables, and return addresses.

2. Flash Memory

Flash memory is a type of non-volatile memory used to store code and other data that needs to persist even when the power is turned off. Flash memory is slower than SRAM but is much more cost-effective for storing large amounts of data in embedded systems.

Key Characteristics of Flash Memory:

- **Non-Volatile**: Retains data even when the power is off.
- **Read/Write Limits**: Flash memory has a limited number of read/write cycles before it starts to degrade, typically

in the range of 10,000 to 1,000,000 cycles, depending on the type of flash.

- **Slow Write Speed**: Writing to flash is slower than reading from it, which must be considered in applications that require frequent writing.

Applications of Flash Memory:

- **Program storage**: Flash memory is commonly used to store the firmware (code) of embedded systems.
- **Data storage**: Flash memory can be used to store configuration settings, log files, or non-volatile variables that should persist across reboots.

3. EEPROM (Electrically Erasable Programmable Read-Only Memory)

EEPROM is another type of non-volatile memory. It allows for byte-level read and write operations, which makes it useful for storing small amounts of data that need to persist across reboots but don't require the large storage capacity of flash memory.

Key Characteristics of EEPROM:

- **Non-Volatile**: Like flash, EEPROM retains its data without power.

- **Byte-Level Write**: Unlike flash, EEPROM allows individual bytes to be written or modified, which makes it more flexible for small data storage needs.
- **Limited Write Cycles**: EEPROMs also have a limited number of write cycles (typically around 1,000,000 cycles), so they are best suited for data that doesn't change frequently.

Applications of EEPROM:

- **Storing configuration data**: Useful for storing settings that should be retained across power cycles, such as calibration data, user settings, or device identification numbers.
- **Log files**: Storing small logs that accumulate over time.

Efficient Memory Management Techniques for Embedded Applications

Effective memory management in embedded systems is essential for ensuring that applications run efficiently without running out of memory or causing system instability. Here are several techniques for managing memory effectively in embedded applications:

1. Memory Partitioning

In embedded systems, memory is often limited, so it is important to partition it effectively to allocate resources where they are needed most. For example:

- **Program code** is stored in **flash memory**, where it is usually read-only.
- **Stack** and **heap** are typically stored in **SRAM**.
- **Persistent data** that needs to survive resets, like configuration parameters, is stored in **EEPROM** or **flash memory**.

By partitioning memory this way, the system ensures that each type of data has the appropriate storage area, and memory is used more efficiently.

2. Dynamic Memory Allocation (Heap Management)

In many embedded systems, dynamic memory allocation is used to allocate and free memory at runtime. This is typically done through **malloc()** and **free()** in C or similar functions in other languages.

Key Considerations:

- **Fragmentation**: Over time, as memory is allocated and freed, the heap can become fragmented. This can result in inefficient use of memory and even memory exhaustion if large blocks are requested and the available memory is scattered.
- **Memory Pools**: One way to manage heap memory more efficiently is through the use of **memory pools**. Memory pools allow you to allocate memory in fixed-size blocks, reducing fragmentation and improving predictability.
- **Garbage Collection**: Some RTOS environments may include garbage collection or explicit memory management tools to monitor and reclaim unused memory.

3. Static Memory Allocation

In many embedded systems, especially those with strict real-time requirements, **static memory allocation** is preferred. This means that memory is allocated at compile-time rather than runtime, which ensures better predictability and reduces the risk of fragmentation.

Benefits of Static Allocation:

- **Deterministic behavior**: Since the memory is pre-allocated, the system knows exactly how much memory is available at any given time.

- **No dynamic overhead**: There is no need to manage dynamic memory, which reduces complexity and avoids runtime allocation errors.

How to Implement:

- Use **global variables**, **local variables**, and **arrays** allocated in the data or BSS sections for static memory.
- Use **buffers** and **queues** with fixed sizes, and allocate them at compile-time.

4. Efficient Use of Stack Memory

Stack memory is used for storing local variables and function call information (e.g., return addresses). Since stack memory is limited in embedded systems, it's important to manage it carefully:

- **Avoid deep recursion**: Recursion consumes a significant amount of stack space. Where possible, replace recursion with iterative algorithms.
- **Minimize local variables**: Use only necessary local variables in functions to reduce stack usage.
- **Use stack size monitoring**: In some RTOS environments, it's possible to monitor stack usage and detect if a stack overflow is imminent.

5. Memory-Mapped I/O and Direct Access

In embedded systems, especially when working with hardware, it's often necessary to access memory-mapped I/O devices directly. Efficient memory management in such systems requires careful control over memory accesses and optimally mapping peripheral registers into the system's memory address space.

Techniques:

- **Direct Memory Access (DMA)**: For data-heavy tasks, DMA can be used to transfer data between peripherals and memory without the CPU's intervention, freeing up CPU cycles for other tasks.
- **Memory-mapped registers**: Direct access to hardware peripherals is achieved using memory-mapped I/O. By using pointers to these memory locations, you can quickly and efficiently access hardware registers.

6. Memory Efficiency in Embedded Operating Systems (RTOS)

When using an RTOS, memory management becomes even more important due to the multitasking nature of these systems. An RTOS typically uses a **memory management unit (MMU)** for managing tasks' memory spaces. To optimize memory:

- **Task stack size**: Set an appropriate stack size for each task. Too large a stack wastes memory, while too small a stack can lead to stack overflows.
- **Kernel memory**: The kernel may require memory for managing tasks, queues, and buffers. Carefully configure memory allocation for the RTOS kernel.

7. Using External Memory (if available)

For systems with limited internal memory, external memory such as SD cards, external flash, or RAM modules can be used to supplement the system's internal memory. Techniques for managing external memory include:

- **Buffering**: Use memory buffers to efficiently manage external memory and prevent data loss during high-speed operations.
- **Data Compression**: For applications like logging or data storage, consider using compression algorithms to store more data in limited external memory.

Conclusion

Efficient memory management is essential in embedded systems, where resources are often limited and time constraints are strict. By understanding the various types of memory used in embedded systems (SRAM, Flash,

EEPROM), and employing memory management techniques such as partitioning, static allocation, and stack management, developers can ensure the optimal performance and reliability of their applications. Moreover, RTOS environments provide mechanisms for managing memory dynamically, making it possible to create sophisticated, real-time applications while maintaining system stability and performance. Efficient memory usage not only prevents crashes and slowdowns but also contributes to the longevity and robustness of embedded systems.

CHAPTER 15

POWER MANAGEMENT IN EMBEDDED SYSTEMS

Power Consumption and Strategies to Optimize It

Power consumption is one of the most important considerations in embedded systems, especially for battery-powered devices or systems that need to operate in remote or energy-constrained environments. Power management techniques are essential for extending the lifespan of embedded systems, improving their efficiency, and ensuring they meet their operational goals.

Embedded systems often consist of multiple components (e.g., sensors, microcontrollers, wireless modules) that can consume power in varying amounts depending on the task being performed. To optimize power consumption, the system must minimize the use of power-hungry components and employ techniques to reduce power when the system is idle or performing non-critical tasks.

Key Factors Affecting Power Consumption:

1. **Microcontroller Power Consumption**:
   - **Active Mode**: In active mode, the microcontroller is executing instructions, and its power consumption depends on the clock frequency, core voltage, and the number of tasks being executed.
   - **Idle Mode**: Even when the microcontroller is not doing significant computation, it may still consume power due to peripherals, clock generation, and background processes.
2. **Peripheral Power Consumption**:
   - Sensors, displays, wireless modules, and actuators can draw significant power, especially when they are continuously active. Managing their power usage is critical.
3. **Communication Modules**:
   - Wireless communication protocols such as **Wi-Fi**, **Bluetooth**, or **LoRa** can be power-hungry when transmitting data over long distances. These modules often have different operating states (e.g., transmit, receive, idle) that consume varying amounts of power.
4. **Clock System**:

- The clock system of an embedded device (oscillator, PLLs, etc.) can significantly impact power consumption. Faster clock speeds typically result in higher power consumption, and slower clock speeds reduce it.

Strategies to Optimize Power Consumption:

1. **Dynamic Voltage and Frequency Scaling (DVFS)**:
   - DVFS is a technique that allows adjusting the operating voltage and frequency of the processor based on workload demands. When the system needs less computational power, the voltage and frequency can be reduced to save energy.
2. **Task Scheduling**:
   - Power management can be improved by scheduling high-power tasks during periods when the system is least likely to affect performance, and by letting low-power tasks run during idle times.
3. **Efficient Use of Peripherals**:
   - Disable unused peripherals (e.g., timers, ADCs, communication interfaces) to reduce unnecessary power consumption. For example, turning off the UART or I2C interface when not in use.
4. **Optimized Code**:

- Efficient algorithms and optimized code can minimize the time the processor spends executing tasks. For instance, reducing the frequency of polling operations and using event-driven programming to minimize CPU usage.

5. **Use of Power-Efficient Components**:
   - Choosing power-efficient components such as low-power microcontrollers, sensors, and wireless communication modules (e.g., BLE instead of Wi-Fi) can reduce overall system power consumption.

Using Sleep Modes and Low-Power Techniques

One of the most effective ways to reduce power consumption in embedded systems is to take advantage of the various **sleep modes** and low-power techniques that modern microcontrollers offer. Most microcontrollers include different sleep modes that reduce their power consumption by selectively disabling certain components and reducing clock speeds.

1. Sleep Modes in Microcontrollers

Microcontrollers often have several different **sleep modes** that allow them to balance between performance and power consumption. These modes typically include:

1. **Active Mode**:
   - The microcontroller operates at full speed, executing instructions and using all its resources. This mode consumes the most power.
2. **Idle Mode**:
   - The microcontroller is not executing code but still keeps the clock running, allowing it to wake up quickly from external interrupts. Some internal peripherals may remain active in this mode, but the CPU itself is idle.
3. **Sleep Mode**:
   - In this mode, most of the microcontroller's peripherals are turned off, and the system operates at a reduced clock frequency. This mode can be used when the system is waiting for an event or when no processing is required. The microcontroller can be woken up by external interrupts or internal timers.
4. **Deep Sleep / Standby Mode**:

- This is a low-power state where most of the microcontroller's functions are disabled, including the clock, CPU, and most peripherals. The system can be woken up from deep sleep through a specific external event or interrupt. This mode consumes the least amount of power but also has the longest wake-up time.

5. **Shutdown Mode**:
   - In shutdown mode, the microcontroller consumes the least amount of power, turning off most of its components. However, it cannot perform any task until it is fully powered up again.

2. Implementing Sleep Modes in Code

Let's see how to implement sleep modes in an embedded system using a microcontroller (e.g., an ARM Cortex-M processor with an RTOS such as FreeRTOS).

c

```
#include "stm32f4xx.h"   // Example for STM32
microcontroller
#include "FreeRTOS.h"
#include "task.h"

void vTask1(void *pvParameters) {
    while (1) {
```

```
        // Perform a task (e.g., toggle LED)
        GPIOB->ODR ^= GPIO_PIN_0;  // Toggle LED
on pin 0
        vTaskDelay(1000 / portTICK_PERIOD_MS);
// Delay for 1 second
    }
}

void vTask2(void *pvParameters) {
    while (1) {
        // Perform another task (e.g., read
sensor data)
        int sensor_data = read_sensor();
        vTaskDelay(500 / portTICK_PERIOD_MS);
// Delay for 500 ms
    }
}

void enter_sleep_mode() {
    // Put the MCU into sleep mode
    __WFI();  // Wait For Interrupt instruction,
puts the MCU into sleep mode
}

int main(void) {
    // Initialize the hardware (GPIO,
peripherals, etc.)
    HAL_Init();
```

```
    __HAL_RCC_GPIOB_CLK_ENABLE();      // Enable
GPIOB clock

    // Create FreeRTOS tasks
    xTaskCreate(vTask1, "Task1", 128, NULL, 1,
NULL);
    xTaskCreate(vTask2, "Task2", 128, NULL, 1,
NULL);

    // Start FreeRTOS scheduler
    vTaskStartScheduler();

    // The system should never reach here
    while (1) {
        enter_sleep_mode();  // Enter sleep mode
to save power
    }
}
```

Explanation:

- **vTask1() and vTask2()**: These are simple tasks created in FreeRTOS. Task 1 toggles an LED, and Task 2 reads sensor data.
- **enter_sleep_mode()**: This function uses the `__WFI()` (Wait For Interrupt) instruction, which puts the microcontroller into a low-power state (sleep mode) while waiting for an interrupt.

- **vTaskDelay()**: A FreeRTOS function used to add delays between task executions, allowing the microcontroller to enter low-power states between tasks.

3. Low-Power Techniques

In addition to using sleep modes, several other techniques can be employed to further optimize power consumption in embedded systems:

1. **Peripheral Power Management**:
   - Disable unused peripherals, such as UART, I2C, SPI, ADC, and PWM, when they are not needed. For example, if your system does not require communication, turning off the UART or I2C module will save power.
2. **Clock Gating**:
   - Clock gating is a technique where the clock signal is turned off for unused components or peripherals. Without a clock, the peripheral consumes minimal power.
3. **Dynamic Voltage Scaling (DVS)**:
   - Dynamically reduce the voltage supplied to the system when the workload is low. Lower voltage generally results in reduced power consumption, although it may also reduce the performance of the system.

4. **Use of Low-Power Components**:
   - Choose components (such as microcontrollers, sensors, and communication modules) that are optimized for low-power consumption. Many modern microcontrollers, for example, include ultra-low-power modes that allow for very low current draw.
5. **Event-Driven Programming**:
   - Use interrupt-driven or event-driven programming models to reduce the need for continuous polling. By responding only when an interrupt or event occurs, the system can remain in low-power states until required to wake up and process events.
6. **Low-Power Communication Protocols**:
   - If your embedded system uses wireless communication, choose low-power communication protocols such as **Bluetooth Low Energy (BLE)** or **LoRaWAN**. These protocols are designed for low-power, long-range communication and are ideal for battery-operated devices.

Conclusion

Power management is essential in embedded systems, especially those with limited resources or battery-powered applications. By understanding the different types of memory and components that affect power consumption, and using efficient power management techniques such as sleep modes, dynamic voltage scaling, and peripheral power management, embedded systems can operate more efficiently and extend battery life. Incorporating these techniques into your system design will ensure that your embedded devices remain reliable, long-lasting, and energy-efficient, even in the most power-constrained environments.

CHAPTER 16

REAL-TIME CLOCK (RTC) AND DATE/TIME MANAGEMENT

Using Real-Time Clocks in Embedded Systems

A **Real-Time Clock (RTC)** is a crucial component in many embedded systems that need to keep track of time accurately. An RTC is a timekeeping device that provides the current time (hours, minutes, seconds) and often the date (day, month, year). Unlike the microcontroller's system clock, which is typically used to keep the processor running, an RTC keeps track of time continuously, even when the system is powered off, thanks to its internal battery.

In embedded systems, RTCs are typically used for applications like:

- **Timestamping**: Recording events or sensor data with precise timestamps.
- **Scheduling**: Triggering actions or events at specific times (e.g., waking up the system at a given time).
- **Timekeeping**: Maintaining accurate time and date for system logs, alarms, and scheduling tasks.

Key Features of an RTC:

1. **Continuous Timekeeping**: RTCs use a dedicated clock (often a crystal oscillator) to maintain time even during system resets or power-down periods.
2. **Battery Backup**: Most RTCs include a small battery (e.g., coin cell battery) to keep running when the main system power is off.
3. **Low Power Consumption**: RTCs are designed to operate with minimal power consumption, which is essential for battery-powered systems.
4. **Accuracy**: RTCs are usually quite accurate, with error rates in the range of seconds per day, but external factors (temperature, voltage) can affect their performance.
5. **Date Management**: RTCs can store and provide the current date (year, month, day) and time (hour, minute, second).

Commonly Used RTC Chips:

- **DS1307**: A popular I2C RTC with low power consumption and integrated battery backup.
- **PCF8523**: A more advanced RTC that offers a higher precision and additional features.
- **MSP430 RTC**: A real-time clock feature built into certain Texas Instruments microcontrollers.

Handling Time-Sensitive Operations with C

When working with time-sensitive operations in embedded systems, the RTC provides a reliable source of time that can be used to manage tasks, schedule events, or timestamp data. In this section, we'll explore how to interface with an RTC in C and handle time-sensitive operations in embedded systems.

1. Interfacing with an RTC Using I2C

In many embedded systems, the RTC is connected via I2C (Inter-Integrated Circuit), a popular communication protocol in embedded systems due to its simplicity and flexibility.

Let’s assume that we are working with the **DS1307 RTC** chip, which communicates over the I2C protocol.

I2C Protocol Overview:

- **SDA (Serial Data)**: Carries data between the microcontroller and the RTC.
- **SCL (Serial Clock)**: Carries the clock signal to synchronize data transfers.

2. Using I2C to Communicate with the RTC

To interact with the RTC, we need to configure the I2C communication, read data from the RTC, and write data to it. The RTC stores the time in **BCD (Binary-Coded Decimal)** format, so we will need to convert it to a standard decimal format for easier processing.

Example: Interfacing with the DS1307 RTC Using I2C in C

```
c

#include <avr/io.h>
#include <util/twi.h>
#include <stdio.h>

#define RTC_ADDRESS 0xD0   // DS1307 I2C address
(write mode)

// Function to initialize the I2C interface
void i2c_init() {
    TWBR = 32;              // Set the clock rate
for I2C (SCL frequency)
    TWSR = 0x00;            // Set prescaler to 1
    TWCR = (1 << TWEN);     // Enable TWI (I2C)
}
```

```
// Function to start I2C communication
void i2c_start() {
    TWCR = (1 << TWSTA) | (1 << TWINT) | (1 <<
TWEN);  // Send start condition
    while (!(TWCR & (1 << TWINT)));  // Wait for
the start condition to finish
}

// Function to stop I2C communication
void i2c_stop() {
    TWCR = (1 << TWSTO) | (1 << TWINT) | (1 <<
TWEN);  // Send stop condition
    while (TWCR & (1 << TWSTO));  // Wait for
stop condition to finish
}

// Function to send a byte of data over I2C
void i2c_write(uint8_t data) {
    TWDR = data;                          // Load the
data byte to send
    TWCR = (1 << TWINT) | (1 << TWEN); // Start
the transmission
    while (!(TWCR & (1 << TWINT)));  // Wait for
the transmission to finish
}

// Function to read a byte of data from I2C
uint8_t i2c_read_ack() {
```

```
    TWCR = (1 << TWINT) | (1 << TWEN) | (1 <<
TWEA);  // Read with acknowledge
    while (!(TWCR & (1 << TWINT)));  // Wait for
the data to be received
    return TWDR;  // Return the received data
}

// Function to read the time from the DS1307 RTC
void   rtc_read_time(uint8_t   *hours,   uint8_t
*minutes, uint8_t *seconds) {
    i2c_start();                     // Start I2C
communication
    i2c_write(RTC_ADDRESS);          // Send RTC
address (write)
    i2c_write(0x00);                 // Point to
the seconds register (0x00)

    i2c_start();                   // Restart the
I2C communication (repeated start)
    i2c_write(RTC_ADDRESS | 0x01); // Send RTC
address (read mode)

    *seconds = i2c_read_ack();    // Read seconds
    *minutes = i2c_read_ack();    // Read minutes
    *hours = i2c_read_ack();        // Read hours

    i2c_stop();                              // End
communication
}
```

```
int main() {
    uint8_t hours, minutes, seconds;

    i2c_init();  // Initialize I2C

    while (1) {
        rtc_read_time(&hours,          &minutes,
&seconds);  // Read time from RTC

        // Display the current time (for example,
using a UART or an LCD)
        printf("Time: %02d:%02d:%02d\n", hours,
minutes, seconds);

        _delay_ms(1000);  // Delay for 1 second
    }

    return 0;
}
```

Explanation:

1. **i2c_init()**: Initializes the I2C interface by setting the clock rate and enabling the TWI (I2C) peripheral.
2. **i2c_start()**: Sends the start condition to initiate communication with the RTC.
3. **i2c_write()**: Sends a byte of data to the RTC.
4. **i2c_read_ack()**: Reads a byte from the RTC with an acknowledgment.

CHAPTER 17

SENSORS AND ACTUATORS IN EMBEDDED SYSTEMS

Interfacing with Sensors (e.g., Temperature, Humidity, Motion)

In embedded systems, sensors are used to detect physical quantities (such as temperature, humidity, or motion) and convert them into electrical signals that the microcontroller can process. Sensors play a vital role in enabling embedded systems to interact with their environment, collect data, and make decisions based on that data.

1. Types of Sensors in Embedded Systems

Here are some common types of sensors used in embedded systems:

1. **Temperature Sensors**:
   - **LM35**: A widely used temperature sensor that provides a linear output voltage proportional to the temperature in Celsius.
   - **DHT11/DHT22**: These are common sensors used to measure both temperature and humidity.
2. **Humidity Sensors**:

- **DHT11/DHT22**: These sensors can measure both temperature and humidity, making them ideal for environmental monitoring.
- **HDC1080**: A more accurate and precise humidity and temperature sensor with digital output.

3. **Motion Sensors**:
    - **PIR (Passive Infrared) Sensors**: Used to detect motion by measuring changes in infrared light levels (e.g., for presence detection in security systems).
    - **Accelerometers and Gyroscopes**: These sensors measure movement and orientation, often used in applications like wearable devices or robotic systems.

2. Interfacing with Sensors

Let's discuss how to interface with these sensors in embedded systems. We'll focus on a temperature and humidity sensor (DHT11) and an accelerometer (ADXL345) for demonstration purposes.

Example 1: Interfacing with a DHT11 Temperature and Humidity Sensor (Using I2C)

The DHT11 sensor provides both temperature and humidity data through a digital output. To read from the sensor, we need to communicate with it using a digital protocol (not I2C or SPI), but the principle is similar for other types of sensors with I2C/SPI communication.

Steps to interface with the DHT11 sensor:

- Connect the DHT11 sensor to the GPIO pin of the microcontroller.
- Use the `DHT` library (available for various microcontrollers) to send and receive data from the sensor.

c

```
#include <dht.h>  // Include the library for DHT sensor

#define DHT_PIN 2  // GPIO pin connected to DHT11 sensor

dht DHT;  // Declare an object to represent the DHT sensor

void setup() {
    Serial.begin(9600);   // Initialize serial communication
    DHT.begin(DHT_PIN);   // Initialize DHT11 sensor on the defined pin
}
```

```
void loop() {
    int humidity = DHT.readHumidity();   // Read
humidity
    int temperature = DHT.readTemperature();   //
Read temperature

    if (humidity == DHT_ERROR || temperature ==
DHT_ERROR) {
        Serial.println("Error    reading    DHT
sensor");
    } else {
        Serial.print("Humidity: ");
        Serial.print(humidity);
        Serial.print("%  Temperature: ");
        Serial.print(temperature);
        Serial.println("°C");
    }

    delay(2000);   // Wait for 2 seconds before
reading again
}
```

Explanation:

- The **DHT** library simplifies interfacing with the DHT11 sensor. The `readHumidity()` and `readTemperature()` functions are used to retrieve the sensor data.

- **Serial.println()** is used to output the data to the serial monitor for debugging.

Example 2: Interfacing with an ADXL345 Accelerometer (Using I2C)

The **ADXL345** is a 3-axis accelerometer that communicates over the I2C interface. It measures acceleration in the x, y, and z directions, which is useful for detecting motion or orientation changes.

Here's a simple example of reading accelerometer data using I2C:

```c
#include <Wire.h>
#include <Adafruit_Sensor.h>
#include <Adafruit_ADXL345_U.h>

Adafruit_ADXL345_Unified accel =
Adafruit_ADXL345_Unified(12345);

void setup() {
    Serial.begin(9600);  // Initialize serial
communication
    if (!accel.begin()) {
```

```
        Serial.println("Couldn't find ADXL345 sensor");
        while (1);
    }
    accel.setRange(ADXL345_RANGE_16G);   // Set the range for the accelerometer
}

void loop() {
    sensors_event_t event;
    accel.getEvent(&event);   // Get the latest accelerometer data

    Serial.print("X: ");
    Serial.print(event.acceleration.x);
    Serial.print("  Y: ");
    Serial.print(event.acceleration.y);
    Serial.print("  Z: ");
    Serial.println(event.acceleration.z);

    delay(1000);  // Wait for 1 second before the next reading
}
```

Explanation:

- The **Adafruit_ADXL345_U** library is used for the ADXL345 accelerometer, which simplifies reading data from the sensor.

- The `getEvent()` function retrieves the accelerometer data, which is then printed to the serial monitor for debugging.

Controlling Actuators (e.g., Motors, Relays)

Actuators are devices that convert electrical signals into physical actions. In embedded systems, actuators such as **motors** and **relays** are used to perform tasks such as driving a robot, controlling the position of a robotic arm, or switching on/off external devices like lights or fans.

1. Types of Actuators

- **Motors**:
  - **DC motors**: Commonly used for driving wheels, fans, or small robotic arms.
  - **Stepper motors**: Used for precise movement control, such as in 3D printers or CNC machines.
  - **Servo motors**: Used for controlling angular position, typically in robotic arms or cameras.
- **Relays**:
  - A relay is an electrically operated switch that can control high-voltage circuits with low-voltage signals. It is typically used to switch devices like lights, motors, or heaters on or off.

2. Controlling Motors

To control a motor, a **motor driver** is typically used, as most microcontrollers cannot provide the required current directly. A popular motor driver is the **L298N**, which allows control of DC motors and stepper motors.

Example: Controlling a DC Motor Using an L298N Motor Driver

c

```
#define IN1 3  // Motor input pin 1
#define IN2 4  // Motor input pin 2
#define ENA 5  // Motor enable pin (PWM control)

void setup() {
    pinMode(IN1, OUTPUT);
    pinMode(IN2, OUTPUT);
    pinMode(ENA, OUTPUT);
}

void loop() {
    // Forward motion
    digitalWrite(IN1, HIGH);
    digitalWrite(IN2, LOW);
    analogWrite(ENA, 255);  // Full speed
    delay(2000);  // Move forward for 2 seconds
```

```
    // Reverse motion
    digitalWrite(IN1, LOW);
    digitalWrite(IN2, HIGH);
    analogWrite(ENA, 255);  // Full speed
    delay(2000);  // Move backward for 2 seconds

    // Stop motion
    analogWrite(ENA, 0);  // Disable motor
    delay(1000);  // Stop for 1 second
}
```

Explanation:

- The L298N motor driver allows the motor's direction to be controlled via two input pins (IN1 and IN2). The **ENA** pin is used to control the motor's speed using PWM (pulse-width modulation).
- The `analogWrite()` function sets the speed, while the `digitalWrite()` function sets the direction.

3. Controlling Relays

Relays are used to control high-power devices with a microcontroller's low-power digital output. A relay module typically includes a transistor and a diode to protect the microcontroller from voltage spikes.

Example: Controlling a Relay to Switch a Light On/Off

```c
#define RELAY_PIN 7  // Relay control pin

void setup() {
    pinMode(RELAY_PIN, OUTPUT);  // Set relay pin
as output
}

void loop() {
    digitalWrite(RELAY_PIN, HIGH);   // Activate
relay (turn on the light)
    delay(5000);  // Wait for 5 seconds
    digitalWrite(RELAY_PIN, LOW);   // Deactivate
relay (turn off the light)
    delay(5000);  // Wait for 5 seconds
}
```

Explanation:

- The relay is controlled by sending a HIGH signal to the relay control pin, which energizes the relay and turns on the connected device (e.g., a light).
- The `delay()` function is used to turn the relay on for 5 seconds and then off for 5 seconds.

Conclusion

In this chapter, we explored how to interface with **sensors** and **actuators** in embedded systems. Sensors like temperature, humidity, and motion detectors allow the system to gather real-world data, while actuators like motors and relays enable the system to interact with the environment by performing physical actions. We discussed common types of sensors and actuators, and provided examples of how to interface with them using embedded C, making it easy to integrate sensors and actuators into real-world embedded applications. Effective integration of these components enables the creation of interactive, responsive, and intelligent systems that can perform tasks autonomously.

CHAPTER 18

COMMUNICATION PROTOCOLS: BLUETOOTH AND WI-FI

Overview of Bluetooth and Wi-Fi in Embedded Systems

Wireless communication is an essential part of modern embedded systems. With the increasing demand for remote monitoring, data exchange, and wireless control, communication protocols like **Bluetooth** and **Wi-Fi** have become integral to embedded systems design. These protocols allow embedded devices to communicate with other devices such as smartphones, computers, or other embedded systems over short or long distances.

1. Bluetooth in Embedded Systems

Bluetooth is a short-range wireless communication protocol that operates on the 2.4 GHz ISM band. It is widely used in applications such as wireless peripherals (e.g., keyboards, mice), audio devices (e.g., headphones, speakers), and IoT devices. Bluetooth is ideal for short-range communication (typically up to 100 meters) and low-power consumption, which makes it suitable for battery-operated embedded devices.

Key Features of Bluetooth:

- **Short-range communication**: Typically ranges from 10 meters to 100 meters, depending on the Bluetooth version.
- **Low power consumption**: Especially in **Bluetooth Low Energy (BLE)**, which is designed for low-power applications like fitness trackers, smartwatches, and medical devices.
- **Point-to-point and multipoint communication**: Bluetooth supports one-to-one (point-to-point) and one-to-many (multipoint) communication, allowing devices like smartphones to communicate with multiple peripherals simultaneously.
- **Security**: Bluetooth offers various security features like encryption and pairing mechanisms to ensure secure communication.

Bluetooth technology has evolved from **Classic Bluetooth** (used for devices like headsets and speakers) to **Bluetooth Low Energy (BLE)**, which focuses on low power consumption and is commonly used in IoT applications.

2. Wi-Fi in Embedded Systems

Wi-Fi is a wireless networking technology that allows devices to connect to the internet or local area networks (LANs) over short to medium distances. It operates on the 2.4 GHz and 5 GHz bands and offers much higher data transfer speeds than Bluetooth, making it suitable for applications that require high-bandwidth communication, such as streaming, web browsing, and cloud-based data exchange.

Key Features of Wi-Fi:

- **Longer range and higher data rates**: Wi-Fi has a range of up to 100 meters indoors and supports higher data rates (up to several hundred Mbps), making it ideal for data-intensive applications.
- **Networked communication**: Wi-Fi enables devices to connect to the internet or local networks, allowing them to interact with cloud services, servers, or other devices on the same network.
- **Security**: Wi-Fi uses various security protocols like WPA2 (Wi-Fi Protected Access) and WPA3 to ensure secure communication.
- **Infrastructure and ad-hoc modes**: Wi-Fi can operate in infrastructure mode (connecting to a router or access

point) or ad-hoc mode (directly connecting to other devices without a router).

Wi-Fi is ideal for applications such as **home automation**, **remote control systems**, and **IoT devices** that require internet connectivity or larger data transfer capabilities.

Programming Microcontrollers for Wireless Communication

In this section, we'll explore how to interface microcontrollers with Bluetooth and Wi-Fi modules to enable wireless communication in embedded systems.

1. Bluetooth Programming in Embedded Systems

To communicate with Bluetooth-enabled devices, microcontrollers often use Bluetooth modules like the **HC-05** (Classic Bluetooth) or **HM-10** (Bluetooth Low Energy, BLE). These modules communicate with the microcontroller over **UART** (Universal Asynchronous Receiver-Transmitter) or **Serial** communication.

Example: Interfacing a Microcontroller with a Bluetooth Module (HC-05)

The HC-05 is a popular Bluetooth module that supports **Serial Communication**. Here's a simple example using the

Arduino platform to send and receive data between a Bluetooth module and a smartphone.

Arduino Code: Sending Data via Bluetooth (HC-05)

```c
#include <SoftwareSerial.h>

// Define the Bluetooth serial pins
SoftwareSerial BTSerial(10, 11); // RX, TX pins for Bluetooth communication

void setup() {
  // Initialize hardware serial communication
  Serial.begin(9600);    // Start the serial monitor communication at 9600 baud rate
  BTSerial.begin(9600); // Start the Bluetooth serial communication at 9600 baud rate

  Serial.println("Bluetooth communication initialized!");
}

void loop() {
  if (BTSerial.available()) {
    // If Bluetooth data is available, send it to the serial monitor
    char data = BTSerial.read();
```

```
    Serial.print(data);   // Print received data
on the serial monitor
  }

  if (Serial.available()) {
    // If data is received from the serial
monitor, send it via Bluetooth
    char data = Serial.read();
    BTSerial.print(data);  // Send the data over
Bluetooth
  }
}
```

Explanation:

- **SoftwareSerial**: This library allows the Arduino to communicate with the Bluetooth module (HC-05) on any two digital pins, such as pins 10 and 11.
- **BTSerial.begin()**: Initializes Bluetooth communication at 9600 baud rate.
- The Arduino reads data from either the Bluetooth module or the serial monitor and sends it to the other device via Bluetooth or USB.

Interfacing with Bluetooth Low Energy (BLE) with the HM-10: The **HM-10** module is used for BLE communication. To communicate with the HM-10, you can use the same approach as above (with `SoftwareSerial`) but make sure that the communication is handled using **BLE profiles** for devices like smartphones.

2. Wi-Fi Programming in Embedded Systems

To enable Wi-Fi connectivity, microcontrollers like the **ESP8266** or **ESP32** are often used. These microcontrollers have built-in Wi-Fi capabilities and are widely used in IoT applications. The **ESP8266** is typically programmed using the **Arduino IDE**, and the **ESP32** offers more advanced features (like Bluetooth and Wi-Fi simultaneously) and better performance.

Example: Interfacing an ESP8266 with Wi-Fi (Arduino)

In this example, we'll connect an **ESP8266** to a Wi-Fi network and send data to a web server (HTTP GET request).

c

```
#include <ESP8266WiFi.h>

// Define Wi-Fi credentials
const char* ssid = "your_SSID";         // Wi-Fi SSID
const char* password = "your_PASSWORD";  // Wi-Fi password
```

```
WiFiClient client;

void setup() {
  Serial.begin(115200);    // Start the serial
communication

  WiFi.begin(ssid, password);  // Connect to the
Wi-Fi network

  while (WiFi.status() != WL_CONNECTED) {   //
Wait until connected
    delay(1000);
    Serial.println("Connecting to WiFi...");
  }

  Serial.println("Connected to WiFi!");
}

void loop() {
  if (client.connect("example.com", 80)) {   //
Connect to a web server (e.g., example.com)
    client.print("GET          /path/to/resource
HTTP/1.1\r\n");
    client.print("Host: example.com\r\n");
    client.print("Connection: close\r\n\r\n");
  }
  delay(5000);  // Wait 5 seconds before making
another request
}
```

Explanation:

- **WiFi.begin()**: Connects the ESP8266 to a Wi-Fi network using the provided SSID and password.
- **client.connect()**: Establishes a connection to a web server (example.com) on port 80 (HTTP).
- **client.print()**: Sends an HTTP GET request to the server.

ESP32 Wi-Fi and Bluetooth Programming: The **ESP32** offers both Wi-Fi and Bluetooth capabilities, which makes it suitable for advanced wireless applications. With the **ESP32**, you can program both Wi-Fi and BLE communication using the same libraries, such as `WiFi.h` for Wi-Fi and `BLEDevice.h` for Bluetooth.

Conclusion

In this chapter, we explored how Bluetooth and Wi-Fi can be used for wireless communication in embedded systems. We covered how to interface microcontrollers with Bluetooth modules like the **HC-05** for Classic Bluetooth communication and how to use **ESP8266** for Wi-Fi connectivity. Both protocols are widely used in embedded systems for applications such as IoT, remote control, and sensor networks. By mastering these wireless communication protocols, you can create embedded systems that communicate seamlessly with other devices over the air, enabling a wide range of exciting and innovative applications.

CHAPTER 19

DEBUGGING EMBEDDED SYSTEMS

Common Debugging Techniques and Tools for Embedded Systems

Debugging is an essential skill for embedded systems developers, as it helps to identify and fix issues in both hardware and software. Embedded systems often present unique challenges due to limited resources, real-time requirements, and tight integration with hardware. However, a systematic debugging approach can significantly improve development efficiency and help resolve issues.

1. Common Debugging Techniques

Here are some standard techniques used to debug embedded systems:

1. **Print Debugging (Serial Output)**:
   - One of the simplest methods of debugging embedded systems is to use **serial communication** to send debugging information to a terminal or PC. By printing variable values, status messages, or error codes to the serial

monitor, developers can trace the flow of the program and identify issues.

   - **Example**: Print sensor values or flags when certain conditions are met. You can also print messages when entering specific functions to check if they are executed.

```c
Serial.begin(9600);
Serial.println("Starting system...");
```

2. **Breakpoints**:
   - **Breakpoints** are markers set within the code that tell the debugger to pause the program execution at that point. Once the program halts, you can inspect the current state of variables, memory, and registers to understand what's going wrong.
   - Breakpoints are commonly used in conjunction with **debugger tools** like GDB (GNU Debugger) or IDEs like **Atmel Studio** and **Eclipse**.
3. **Step-by-Step Execution**:
   - **Single-stepping** allows you to execute code one instruction at a time. This helps observe the flow of the program and see how each line of code affects system state, which is useful for pinpointing logical errors and race conditions.

   - This can be done in most IDE debuggers, and it is helpful in identifying exactly where and how an error happens.
4. **Watchpoints**:
   - A **watchpoint** is a debugging feature that allows you to monitor the value of a specific variable or memory address during execution. When the variable changes (or reaches a certain value), the program will break or pause.
   - Watchpoints are useful for tracking down issues related to variables that are altered unexpectedly or not initialized properly.
5. **Logic Analyzers and Oscilloscopes**:
   - A **logic analyzer** can capture and visualize digital signals in your system. This is particularly useful for monitoring communication protocols like I2C, SPI, or UART, helping you to identify issues in the transmission of data between the microcontroller and peripheral devices.
   - An **oscilloscope** is invaluable for visualizing analog signals, measuring waveforms, and diagnosing issues related to timing or noise in electrical circuits.
6. **Unit Testing and Test Automation**:
   - Writing **unit tests** for individual functions or modules in the embedded software can help catch

bugs early in the development process. **Test automation** frameworks (e.g., **Ceedling, Unity**) are available for embedded systems to automatically execute and verify tests.

- Testing on simulated environments can allow for early bug detection without needing to run the program on the actual hardware.

2. Tools for Debugging Embedded Systems

Various debugging tools can significantly improve the debugging process in embedded systems development:

1. **Integrated Development Environments (IDEs)**:
   - **Keil uVision**, **Atmel Studio**, **Eclipse**, and **Arduino IDE** are widely used in embedded development. These IDEs offer built-in debugging support, such as setting breakpoints, stepping through code, inspecting memory, and using serial communication to output debug information.
   - Some IDEs also provide support for **JTAG** debugging, enabling low-level access to the processor.
2. **JTAG/SWD Debugging**:
   - **JTAG (Joint Test Action Group)** and **SWD (Serial Wire Debug)** are debugging interfaces

that allow low-level access to a microcontroller. Using a **JTAG/SWD debugger** (such as **Segger J-Link** or **ST-Link**), developers can interact with the microcontroller's internal registers and memory during code execution.

- These tools allow you to set breakpoints, watch variables, step through code, and access peripheral registers. They are particularly useful for debugging at the hardware level when the system is running.

3. **GDB (GNU Debugger)**:
    - **GDB** is a powerful command-line debugger commonly used in embedded systems development. GDB can be used with various debuggers, such as **OpenOCD** (Open On-Chip Debugger), to interface with microcontrollers over JTAG or SWD.
    - GDB supports breakpoints, watchpoints, step execution, and allows you to inspect memory and register values while the program is running.
4. **Simulators and Emulators**:
    - **Simulators** emulate the behavior of the microcontroller and allow you to test software before deploying it on hardware. Simulators can run your embedded code without requiring the

actual hardware, providing insights into the program's logic and identifying errors.

- **Emulators**, like **QEMU**, simulate embedded hardware at a higher level and can be used to run and debug code across different microcontroller platforms.

5. **Serial Communication Debugging**:
   - The use of **serial debugging** tools is vital for embedded systems. **Serial-to-USB converters** (such as **FTDI chips** or **USB-to-Serial adapters**) allow communication between a microcontroller and a PC over UART. Serial communication tools, like **PuTTY** or **Tera Term**, can be used to monitor real-time debug information sent from the microcontroller.
6. **Bus Analyzers and Protocol Analyzers**:
   - **I2C/SPI Bus Analyzers** or **CAN analyzers** are tools that allow you to monitor communication between the microcontroller and peripheral devices. These tools can show you the communication signals, making it easier to spot protocol errors, timing issues, or data corruption.

Handling Hardware and Software Issues in Embedded Applications

Debugging embedded systems involves both **hardware** and **software** issues. Many problems arise from the interaction between hardware and software, which makes it necessary to address both aspects during debugging.

1. Hardware Issues

Hardware-related issues can often be difficult to debug, as they may be related to the physical components of the system, such as sensors, power supply, or communication buses. Some common hardware-related issues include:

- **Power Supply Issues**: Insufficient or fluctuating power can cause erratic behavior in embedded systems. Always verify the power supply voltage and check for issues such as noise or voltage drops, especially in battery-powered systems.
    - **Solution**: Use an **oscilloscope** to check for voltage stability, and ensure the power supply can handle the required load.
- **Pin Misconnections**: Incorrect wiring of peripheral devices or microcontroller pins can cause malfunctioning systems.
    - **Solution**: Double-check the pinout of connected components and ensure that signals are correctly routed. Using a **logic analyzer** can help trace data across the system.

- **Signal Integrity Issues**: High-speed signals (e.g., I2C, SPI, UART) can be subject to noise, reflections, or cross-talk between wires, which may lead to data corruption or communication errors.
    - **Solution**: Use **shielded wires** for signal transmission, add **pull-up/pull-down resistors** to I2C or SPI lines, and check the layout of PCB traces.
- **Overheating or Component Failure**: Overheated components (e.g., regulators, transistors, microcontrollers) can cause unpredictable behavior or complete system failure.
    - **Solution**: Measure component temperatures using a **thermal camera** or a **temperature sensor**.

2. Software Issues

Software-related problems can range from simple logical errors in the code to complex issues with real-time task scheduling, memory usage, or peripheral initialization.

- **Memory Corruption**: Embedded systems are often constrained by limited memory. Bugs like buffer overflows, uninitialized variables, or improper memory access can corrupt data and lead to system crashes.

  - **Solution**: Use **watchpoints** to track variable changes, check memory allocation carefully, and use **stack overflow detection** tools if available.

- **Timing and Synchronization Issues**: In real-time systems, timing is crucial. Issues such as task prioritization, improper interrupt handling, or incorrect delays can result in missed deadlines or system instability.
  - **Solution**: Use **RTOS debugging tools** to monitor task execution, check the priority levels of tasks, and use **real-time clocks** for time-sensitive operations.
- **Peripheral Initialization and Configuration**: If peripherals such as sensors, actuators, or communication modules are not correctly initialized, they may not work as expected.
  - **Solution**: Verify peripheral initialization code and check for misconfigured registers or incorrect communication protocols.
- **Concurrency Issues**: Embedded systems often need to handle multiple tasks or processes simultaneously. Issues such as race conditions, deadlocks, or

improper resource access can result in unpredictable behavior.

- **Solution**: Use **semaphores**, **mutexes**, and **event flags** to synchronize tasks in multi-threaded environments. Utilize **task schedulers** to ensure fair task execution.

Conclusion

Debugging embedded systems requires a comprehensive understanding of both hardware and software, as well as the tools available to address issues at different levels. Common techniques like print debugging, breakpoints, and watchpoints, combined with powerful debugging tools such as JTAG debuggers, logic analyzers, and oscilloscopes, can help diagnose and resolve issues efficiently. By addressing both hardware and software concerns, embedded system developers can ensure the reliability, stability, and performance of their applications. With practice and the right tools, debugging becomes a systematic and effective process for delivering high-quality embedded systems.

CHAPTER 20

FIRMWARE DEVELOPMENT AND UPDATE MECHANISMS

Writing and Updating Firmware in Embedded Systems

Firmware is the software embedded into the non-volatile memory of embedded systems, such as microcontrollers or sensors. It directly controls the hardware and allows for specific tasks to be carried out. Writing and updating firmware is an essential skill for embedded system developers, as it enables the creation of applications and the ability to enhance or fix them over time.

1. Writing Firmware for Embedded Systems

Writing firmware for embedded systems typically involves several key steps:

1. **Understanding the Hardware**:
   - Before writing firmware, it is essential to understand the hardware architecture of the system, including the microcontroller, sensors, actuators, communication interfaces, and other peripherals. This knowledge will guide the

initialization of hardware components and their interaction within the system.

2. **Choosing the Right Development Environment**:
   - Embedded firmware is usually written in **C** or **C++**, though assembly language may be used for low-level tasks. Development environments (IDEs) like **Keil uVision**, **Atmel Studio**, or **STM32CubeIDE** provide support for embedded systems programming, offering features like code editing, debugging, and integration with hardware.
3. **Configuring the Microcontroller**:
   - Microcontrollers often have different clock sources, communication protocols (e.g., SPI, I2C, UART), and peripheral initialization requirements. The first step in writing firmware is configuring the microcontroller's system clock, initializing its I/O pins, and setting up communication interfaces.
4. **Firmware Design**:
   - Firmware development follows a structured design process, including:
     - **Initialization**: Set up and configure microcontroller peripherals, such as timers, ADCs, and communication modules.

- **Main Loop**: The main firmware loop is responsible for reading inputs (e.g., sensors), processing data, and sending outputs (e.g., controlling motors, activating relays).
- **Interrupts**: Interrupts are used for real-time processing, such as handling sensor data or responding to button presses.

5. **Writing Device Drivers**:
   - Device drivers are used to interact with hardware components like sensors or actuators. Writing efficient device drivers is key to ensuring smooth communication between the firmware and the hardware.
6. **Testing and Debugging**:
   - Thorough testing of the firmware is critical. Use debugging tools such as **breakpoints**, **serial communication**, and **logic analyzers** to verify that the firmware works as expected. Use **unit tests** where applicable to test individual components of the firmware.

Example: Simple LED Blinking Firmware (Arduino)

c

```
#define LED_PIN 13
```

```
void setup() {
    pinMode(LED_PIN, OUTPUT);  // Initialize the
LED pin as output
}

void loop() {
    digitalWrite(LED_PIN, HIGH);  // Turn the LED
on
    delay(1000);                   // Wait for 1
second
    digitalWrite(LED_PIN, LOW);   // Turn the LED
off
    delay(1000);                   // Wait for 1
second
}
```

Explanation:

- This simple example uses the **Arduino platform** to blink an LED connected to pin 13.
- **setup()** is called once to initialize the pin mode, while the **loop()** runs continuously, turning the LED on and off with a delay.

2. Updating Firmware in Embedded Systems

Updating the firmware in embedded systems is a critical task, especially for devices in the field that need bug fixes or new features. Updating firmware is done in two main ways: **local updates** and **remote updates**.

Local Firmware Updates

Local firmware updates typically involve:

- **Flashing the firmware**: The firmware is reprogrammed using a direct connection to the device (e.g., **USB**, **JTAG**, or **ISP**).
- **Bootloader**: Some embedded systems use a **bootloader** to facilitate local firmware updates. The bootloader resides in a protected section of memory and allows the system to receive new firmware over a communication interface, such as **UART** or **USB**, and flash it into the main memory.

Remote Firmware Updates (OTA)

Remote firmware updates, also known as **Over-the-Air (OTA)** updates, are commonly used in IoT and remote embedded devices. These updates enable devices to receive new firmware versions without needing a physical connection to the development environment, which is especially useful for devices that are deployed in the field.

Techniques for Remote Firmware Updates (OTA)

OTA firmware updates allow embedded systems to receive and apply new firmware versions over a network connection. The process involves several key components, including **firmware storage**, **secure transmission**, and **firmware installation**. There are different methods for implementing OTA updates, depending on the system's requirements and communication capabilities.

1. OTA Update Workflow

The typical OTA update process consists of the following steps:

1. **Check for Updates**:
   - The device periodically checks for available updates by querying a central server or cloud platform (e.g., using **HTTP** or **MQTT** protocols). The server maintains a repository of firmware files and metadata (e.g., version number).
2. **Download the Firmware**:
   - Once an update is available, the device downloads the firmware image from the server over a network (e.g., Wi-Fi or cellular). The

downloaded image is typically stored in non-volatile memory (e.g., **flash** or **SD card**) temporarily.

3. **Validate the Firmware**:
    - Before applying the update, the device verifies the integrity of the firmware file (using **checksums**, **hashing**, or **digital signatures**) to ensure that the firmware is not corrupted or tampered with.
4. **Apply the Update**:
    - After validation, the device enters a **bootloader mode**, which allows the new firmware to be written into the device's primary memory (usually flash memory). This process involves erasing old firmware and writing the new firmware, which can take several seconds or minutes.
5. **Reboot and Run New Firmware**:
    - Once the firmware is updated, the system reboots and starts running the new firmware version. A **fail-safe** mechanism is often included to ensure that if the update fails, the system can revert to the previous working firmware.

2. OTA Implementation Considerations

1. **Secure Firmware Updates**:

- Security is critical for OTA updates to prevent malicious attacks, such as **man-in-the-middle (MITM)** attacks or **malware injection**. Common security measures include:
  - **Encryption**: The firmware should be encrypted during transmission to prevent unauthorized access.
  - **Authentication**: The device must verify the server's identity (using **TLS** or **SSL**) to ensure it is communicating with a trusted source.
  - **Digital Signatures**: The firmware image can be signed using cryptographic techniques to verify its authenticity.

2. **Firmware Size and Efficiency**:
   - Firmware files must be optimized for size, especially in systems with limited memory. **Compression** techniques can help reduce the size of firmware files before transmission.
3. **Version Control and Rollback Mechanisms**:
   - The system should support version control to ensure that the latest firmware is installed. Additionally, it should include a rollback mechanism in case the new firmware causes issues, allowing the device to revert to the previous version if necessary.

4. **Over-the-Air Protocols**:
   - **HTTP/HTTPS** is commonly used for OTA updates because it is widely supported and provides a simple way to fetch firmware from a web server.
   - **MQTT** is used in many IoT applications for sending small payloads with low overhead.
   - **CoAP** and **LwM2M** are lightweight protocols designed for IoT devices, providing efficient communication for firmware updates.

3. Example: Simple OTA Firmware Update Using HTTP (ESP32)

The **ESP32** is a popular Wi-Fi-enabled microcontroller with built-in OTA capabilities. Here's an example of how to implement an OTA update using the **ESP32** platform and **Arduino IDE**.

OTA Update Example Code (ESP32)

c

```
#include <WiFi.h>
#include <HTTPClient.h>
#include <ArduinoOTA.h>

const char* ssid = "your_SSID";
const char* password = "your_PASSWORD";
```

```
void setup() {
  Serial.begin(115200);
  WiFi.begin(ssid, password);

  while (WiFi.status() != WL_CONNECTED) {
    delay(1000);
    Serial.println("Connecting to WiFi...");
  }

  Serial.println("Connected to WiFi");

  // Initialize OTA
  ArduinoOTA.begin();
}

void loop() {
  // Handle OTA updates
  ArduinoOTA.handle();

  // Periodically check for new firmware update
  if (WiFi.status() == WL_CONNECTED) {
    HTTPClient http;

http.begin("http://example.com/firmware_update.
bin");

    int httpCode = http.GET();    // Get the
firmware file from the server
```

```
    if (httpCode == HTTP_CODE_OK) {
      // Proceed with firmware update (write the
file to flash)
      // Use the OTA library to handle the actual
update
      ArduinoOTA.begin();  // Starting the OTA
process
    }

    http.end();
  }

  delay(10000);   // Check every 10 seconds for
updates
}
```

Explanation:

- This example demonstrates how to set up OTA updates on the **ESP32**.
- The microcontroller connects to Wi-Fi, checks for new firmware updates from the server, and uses the **ArduinoOTA** library to apply the update.

Conclusion

In this chapter, we explored the essential topic of **firmware development** and **update mechanisms** in embedded systems. Writing firmware involves configuring hardware, initializing peripherals, and testing software for reliable performance. We also discussed **remote firmware updates (OTA)**, which allow devices to receive and apply new firmware over the air, ensuring that systems can be updated in the field without physical access. Security, version control, and communication protocols are vital for ensuring successful and safe firmware updates. With the right tools and techniques, firmware development and updates become streamlined, enabling embedded systems to remain functional and up-to-date over time.

CHAPTER 21

DESIGN PATTERNS FOR EMBEDDED SYSTEMS

Introduction to Design Patterns for Embedded Systems

Design patterns are established solutions to common software design problems. They provide a proven template for solving recurring challenges in software architecture and ensure code maintainability, scalability, and readability. In embedded systems, where hardware constraints, real-time requirements, and resource limitations are often present, design patterns help create efficient, modular, and flexible systems.

Embedded systems development can benefit from applying the right design patterns to ensure that complex hardware and software interactions are handled effectively. The use of design patterns promotes reusability, reduces redundancy, and improves code clarity, which is especially valuable in embedded systems where debugging and maintenance are crucial.

Why Use Design Patterns in Embedded Systems?

1. **Efficiency**: Embedded systems often have strict constraints on resources, including memory, CPU, and power. Design patterns help structure software to optimize resource usage.
2. **Code Reusability**: Once a pattern is defined, it can be reused across various projects, reducing development time and effort.
3. **Maintainability**: By using well-established design patterns, developers can write code that is easier to maintain and extend, which is essential in long-lived embedded systems.
4. **Scalability**: Embedded systems may need to evolve to handle more peripherals, sensors, or network interfaces. Design patterns provide a flexible framework to accommodate future requirements.

Types of Design Patterns in Embedded Systems

Design patterns are typically classified into three categories:

- **Creational Patterns**: Concerned with the way objects are created, ensuring that the system's object creation is efficient and flexible.
- **Structural Patterns**: Concerned with the organization and composition of objects to form larger structures.

- **Behavioral Patterns**: Focused on communication between objects and the flow of control.

In embedded systems, certain patterns are especially useful due to the nature of the hardware and software interactions. Let's examine a few of the most commonly used design patterns in embedded systems.

1. Creational Patterns in Embedded Systems

Creational patterns focus on the process of object creation, making it more flexible and efficient. In embedded systems, where memory management and resource allocation are critical, these patterns ensure that objects are created optimally.

1.1 Singleton Pattern

The **Singleton Pattern** ensures that a class has only one instance and provides a global point of access to it. In embedded systems, this is useful when a single instance of a resource (e.g., a communication module or hardware driver) is required.

Use Case: A microcontroller's UART or SPI module is often accessed by different parts of the system, but only one instance should be created to avoid conflicts and resource wastage.

Example:

```
c

class UART {
private:
    static UART* instance;

    //   Private   constructor   to   prevent
instantiation
    UART() {}

public:
    static UART* getInstance() {
        if (instance == nullptr) {
            instance = new UART();
        }
        return instance;
    }

    void sendData(uint8_t data) {
        // Send data over UART
    }
};

// Initialize static member
```

```
UART* UART::instance = nullptr;

int main() {
    UART* uart = UART::getInstance();
    uart->sendData(0x55);  // Send data using the
single instance
}
```

Explanation:

- **UART** is designed as a singleton, ensuring only one instance is created.
- This prevents multiple instances of the UART driver from being created, ensuring efficient communication.

1.2 Factory Method Pattern

The **Factory Method Pattern** is used to create objects without specifying the exact class of object that will be created. In embedded systems, this can be used to instantiate different types of peripherals, depending on the hardware configuration or requirements.

Use Case: A factory method might be used to create different types of sensor drivers based on the sensor connected to the system.

Example:

```c
class Sensor {
public:
    virtual void readData() = 0;  // Pure virtual
function
};

class TemperatureSensor : public Sensor {
public:
    void readData() override {
        // Read temperature data
    }
};

class HumiditySensor : public Sensor {
public:
    void readData() override {
        // Read humidity data
    }
};

class SensorFactory {
public:
    static Sensor* createSensor(int type) {
        if (type == 1) {
            return new TemperatureSensor();
        } else if (type == 2) {
            return new HumiditySensor();
```

```
        }
        return nullptr;
    }
};

int main() {
    Sensor*                    sensor                    =
SensorFactory::createSensor(1);    //  Create  a
temperature sensor
    sensor->readData();
    delete sensor;
}
```

Explanation:

- The **SensorFactory** class creates different sensor objects (e.g., **TemperatureSensor** or **HumiditySensor**) based on input parameters.
- This allows for flexible and modular code, enabling different sensors to be added without modifying the core system logic.

2. Structural Patterns in Embedded Systems

Structural patterns deal with how objects and classes are organized to form larger structures. These patterns are particularly useful when the system requires interaction between several hardware components, such as peripherals or communication modules.

2.1 Adapter Pattern

The **Adapter Pattern** allows incompatible interfaces to work together. This is especially helpful in embedded systems when interfacing with various communication protocols or legacy hardware modules.

Use Case: If your system needs to interface with multiple types of communication protocols (e.g., I2C and SPI), the Adapter Pattern can provide a unified interface to manage these protocols.

Example:

```
c

class I2C {
public:
    void communicate() {
        // Communicate via I2C
    }
};

class SPI {
public:
```

```
    void communicate() {
        // Communicate via SPI
    }
};

class CommunicationAdapter {
private:
    I2C* i2c;
    SPI* spi;

public:
    CommunicationAdapter() {
        i2c = new I2C();
        spi = new SPI();
    }

    void communicate(char protocol) {
        if (protocol == 'I') {
            i2c->communicate();
        } else if (protocol == 'S') {
            spi->communicate();
        }
    }
};

int main() {
    CommunicationAdapter adapter;
    adapter.communicate('I');   // Use I2C for
communication
```

```
    adapter.communicate('S');    // Use SPI for
communication
}
```

Explanation:

- **CommunicationAdapter** acts as an interface between different communication protocols (I2C and SPI).
- The system can switch between protocols without needing to modify the rest of the application code.

3. Behavioral Patterns in Embedded Systems

Behavioral patterns focus on the interaction and communication between objects. These patterns are crucial in managing complex processes like task scheduling, real-time data handling, and event-driven programming in embedded systems.

3.1 Observer Pattern

The **Observer Pattern** allows objects (observers) to subscribe to an event or data change in another object (subject). This is particularly useful in embedded systems where multiple components need to respond to changes in sensor data or other events.

Use Case: In a smart thermostat system, the temperature sensor might notify different components (e.g., the display, the heating element) when the temperature changes.

Example:

```c
#include <vector>
#include <iostream>

class Observer {
public:
    virtual void update(int temperature) = 0;
};

class TemperatureSensor {
private:
    std::vector<Observer*> observers;
    int temperature;

public:
    void addObserver(Observer* observer) {
        observers.push_back(observer);
    }

    void setTemperature(int temp) {
        temperature = temp;
        notifyObservers();
```

```
    }

    void notifyObservers() {
        for (Observer* observer : observers) {
            observer->update(temperature);
        }
    }
};

class Display : public Observer {
public:
    void update(int temperature) override {
        std::cout     <<     "Display    updated:
Temperature is " << temperature << "°C\n";
    }
};

class Heater : public Observer {
public:
    void update(int temperature) override {
        if (temperature < 20) {
            std::cout << "Heater turned on\n";
        } else {
            std::cout << "Heater turned off\n";
        }
    }
};

int main() {
```

```
    TemperatureSensor sensor;
    Display display;
    Heater heater;

    sensor.addObserver(&display);
    sensor.addObserver(&heater);

    sensor.setTemperature(18);   // Trigger the
update

    return 0;
}
```

Explanation:

- The **TemperatureSensor** is the **subject** that notifies its **observers** (in this case, the **Display** and **Heater**) whenever the temperature changes.
- This pattern is useful for creating modular, event-driven systems in embedded systems.

Conclusion

In this chapter, we explored several **design patterns** that can be applied to embedded systems development, including **creational**, **structural**, and **behavioral** patterns. These patterns help address common challenges such as efficient resource usage, modularity, and flexible communication between components. By applying these patterns, embedded systems developers can create more scalable, maintainable, and efficient applications, especially in complex systems that involve hardware control, real-time data processing, and communication protocols. Understanding and applying the right design patterns can significantly improve the development process and the quality of embedded systems.

CHAPTER 22

SECURITY IN EMBEDDED SYSTEMS

Security Challenges in Embedded Systems

Security in embedded systems is increasingly important as these systems are being used in critical applications such as healthcare devices, automotive systems, industrial control systems, and smart homes. However, embedded systems present unique security challenges that make them vulnerable to a variety of attacks. Understanding these challenges is essential for designing secure embedded systems that can withstand malicious threats and vulnerabilities.

1. Limited Resources

Many embedded systems have **limited processing power**, **memory**, and **storage** compared to general-purpose computers. These constraints make it challenging to implement traditional security mechanisms like **encryption**, **firewalls**, or **intrusion detection systems** that are common in conventional IT environments.

- **Impact**: Implementing resource-heavy security algorithms may slow down the embedded system, affecting its performance and reliability.
- **Solution**: Lightweight security protocols and encryption algorithms, such as **AES (Advanced Encryption Standard)** with reduced key sizes, can be used to strike a balance between security and performance.

2. Lack of Regular Updates

Unlike traditional computer systems, embedded systems are often deployed in the field for long periods without any mechanism to update their software or firmware. Once deployed, they may not receive timely security patches or updates.

- **Impact**: Systems that are not updated regularly become vulnerable to new threats and exploits.
- **Solution**: **Over-the-Air (OTA)** firmware updates should be implemented so that devices can be updated remotely and securely. Proper update mechanisms must ensure that firmware is authenticated and encrypted before installation to avoid tampering.

3. Physical Access to Devices

Embedded systems are often deployed in environments where physical access is possible, such as in consumer products, industrial machines, and even medical devices. An attacker with physical access to the device can potentially extract sensitive data or modify the firmware.

- **Impact**: Physical access exposes the system to attacks such as **hardware cloning**, **side-channel attacks**, or **reverse engineering**.
- **Solution**: **Tamper-resistant hardware**, **secure boot mechanisms**, and **encryption** can be employed to protect the device against physical attacks.

4. Communication Vulnerabilities

Many embedded systems rely on communication protocols like **I2C**, **SPI**, **UART**, **Bluetooth**, or **Wi-Fi** to interact with other devices or networks. These communication channels can be intercepted or manipulated by attackers if not properly secured.

- **Impact**: Attackers can eavesdrop on or alter the communication between devices, leading to **man-in-the-middle attacks**, **data injection**, or **denial-of-service (DoS)** attacks.

- **Solution**: Secure communication protocols such as **TLS/SSL** (for Wi-Fi or Ethernet) and **Bluetooth Low Energy (BLE)** security should be used to ensure confidentiality, integrity, and authentication during communication.

5. Third-Party Software Components

Embedded systems often use third-party software components, libraries, or modules to implement features like networking, sensor drivers, or user interfaces. These components may contain **vulnerabilities** or **backdoors** that can be exploited by attackers.

- **Impact**: Vulnerabilities in third-party components can expose the system to a wide range of attacks.
- **Solution**: Regular audits and vulnerability scanning of third-party components are crucial to ensure they do not introduce security risks. **Software supply chain security** practices should also be adopted to verify the integrity of third-party code.

Best Practices for Securing Embedded Firmware and Hardware

Securing embedded systems requires a multi-layered approach that addresses both the **firmware** and **hardware** layers of the system. Below are best practices for securing embedded systems against various types of threats.

1. Secure Boot

Secure Boot ensures that only trusted firmware is executed on the embedded system. During the boot process, the firmware is checked against a **cryptographic signature** or **hash** to verify its authenticity and integrity. If the firmware is tampered with, the system will not boot.

- **How It Works**: The bootloader verifies the firmware's signature using a **public key** before loading it into memory. If the signature is invalid, the system halts, preventing malicious code from executing.
- **Benefits**: Secure boot prevents **rootkit** installation and ensures that only authorized firmware is loaded, reducing the risk of malware.

2. Hardware-Based Security

Using **hardware security modules (HSM)** or **trusted platform modules (TPM)** can enhance the security of embedded systems. These components provide **secure storage** for cryptographic keys, passwords, and other sensitive data, making it difficult for attackers to access or tamper with these assets.

- **How It Works**: HSMs and TPMs perform cryptographic operations in a physically isolated environment, ensuring that secret keys never leave the hardware.
- **Benefits**: Secure hardware helps protect sensitive information and cryptographic operations, even if the software or operating system is compromised.

3. Data Encryption

Encrypting sensitive data, both **at rest** (on storage) and **in transit** (during communication), is critical for securing embedded systems. Use **lightweight encryption algorithms** that balance security and resource efficiency, such as **AES** or **ECC (Elliptic Curve Cryptography)**, depending on the system's constraints.

- **How It Works**: Data is encrypted before being stored on the system or sent over communication channels. Only authorized devices or users with the appropriate decryption keys can access the data.
- **Benefits**: Encryption ensures the confidentiality and integrity of data, protecting it from eavesdropping, tampering, and theft.

4. Access Control and Authentication

Implement strict **access control** mechanisms to limit which users or devices can interact with the embedded system. **Authentication** should be used to verify the identity of devices, users, or software components before granting access.

- **How It Works**: Authentication mechanisms, such as **passwords**, **biometrics**, **public key infrastructure (PKI)**, or **tokens**, are used to verify identities. Access control policies limit the permissions granted to each authenticated entity.
- **Benefits**: Access control ensures that only authorized entities can interact with critical system resources, reducing the risk of unauthorized modifications or attacks.

5. Firmware Integrity and Authenticity

To ensure that firmware is not tampered with, use cryptographic methods like **hashing** and **digital signatures**. This ensures that any update or modification to the firmware is verified before it is executed.

- **How It Works**: When firmware is updated, its cryptographic hash or signature is checked against the expected value to verify its authenticity and integrity. Only signed and verified firmware is allowed to execute.

- **Benefits**: This prevents the installation of malicious or unauthorized firmware updates, which could compromise the system's security.

6. Regular Security Patches and Updates

Regularly update the firmware to fix known vulnerabilities and improve security. **Automated firmware updates** via **Over-the-Air (OTA)** mechanisms can help ensure that the latest security patches are applied.

- **How It Works**: The embedded system periodically checks for updates and downloads the latest firmware versions from a secure server. The firmware is then authenticated, verified, and applied to the system.
- **Benefits**: Regular updates ensure that the system remains secure against evolving threats, ensuring that vulnerabilities are patched before they can be exploited.

7. Monitoring and Logging

Enable **logging** and **real-time monitoring** of system activity to detect and respond to potential security breaches. Logs should be stored securely to prevent tampering, and any suspicious activity should trigger an alert for further investigation.

- **How It Works**: Log files store information about system events, errors, and security-related activities. Monitoring tools analyze these logs for unusual patterns or behaviors, such as unauthorized access attempts or buffer overflows.
- **Benefits**: Continuous monitoring helps detect potential security threats early and allows for rapid response to mitigate any damage.

8. Minimize Attack Surface

Reducing the attack surface of an embedded system is one of the most effective ways to improve security. This includes:

- **Disabling unused services**: Turn off unnecessary communication interfaces (e.g., UART, SPI, I2C) and peripherals to limit potential entry points for attackers.
- **Code minimization**: Use only essential code and libraries to reduce the likelihood of vulnerabilities.
- **Network segmentation**: Isolate critical components of the system from less sensitive ones to prevent lateral movement by attackers.

- **How It Works**: The attack surface is minimized by limiting the system's exposure to potential vulnerabilities. This can be done by turning off unused features, reducing the size of the firmware, and using firewall or network security policies.
- **Benefits**: By minimizing the attack surface, the system becomes less vulnerable to attacks and unauthorized access.

Conclusion

Security is a critical aspect of embedded systems, especially as these systems are increasingly integrated into everyday devices and critical infrastructures. Due to their resource constraints, physical accessibility, and communication vulnerabilities, embedded systems face unique security challenges. By adopting security best practices such as **secure boot**, **data encryption**, **hardware-based security**, **firmware integrity checks**, and **OTA updates**, developers can mitigate these risks and create robust, secure systems. Implementing layered security measures, including **access control**, **regular updates**, and **monitoring**, ensures that embedded systems are protected from evolving threats and vulnerabilities.

CHAPTER 23

CASE STUDY: BUILDING A SMART HOME DEVICE

Designing and Developing a Smart Home Device Using Embedded Systems and C

The demand for smart home devices is increasing, as they provide convenience, energy efficiency, and enhanced control over household systems. Embedded systems form the backbone of many smart home devices, allowing them to interact with sensors, control appliances, and communicate over wireless networks. In this chapter, we will walk through the process of designing and developing a smart home device—specifically, a **smart thermostat**—using embedded systems and C programming.

Key Components of a Smart Home Device

Before diving into the design and development process, let's take a look at the key components that will be involved in building a smart thermostat:

1. **Microcontroller**: This is the brain of the thermostat, responsible for processing data from sensors, controlling

the actuators (e.g., a heating element or cooling fan), and communicating with other devices or networks.

2. **Temperature Sensor**: A sensor like the **DHT22** or **LM35** will be used to measure the temperature of the room.
3. **Relay**: A relay will be used to control the heating or cooling system based on the temperature data received from the sensor.
4. **User Interface (UI)**: A small LCD or OLED display will be used to show the current temperature and settings. A set of buttons or a rotary encoder can be used for user input (adjusting the target temperature).
5. **Communication Interface**: The device may include wireless communication (e.g., **Wi-Fi** using the **ESP8266** or **ESP32**) to allow the thermostat to be controlled remotely via a smartphone or other smart devices.
6. **Power Supply**: The device will require a stable power supply to operate the sensors, display, and microcontroller.

Design Considerations

When designing a smart home device like a thermostat, several factors need to be considered:

- **Real-Time Control**: The system must respond to changes in temperature in real-time to turn the heating or cooling system on or off.
- **Low Power Consumption**: Since the thermostat will often run continuously, it is essential to optimize the firmware and hardware for low power consumption.
- **User-Friendly Interface**: The system should have a simple, intuitive interface that allows users to view the current temperature and set desired temperature thresholds.
- **Remote Control**: Ideally, the thermostat should allow users to monitor and control the temperature remotely (via a smartphone app or web interface).
- **Reliability and Accuracy**: The temperature measurement must be accurate, and the system should operate reliably over long periods.

Step-by-Step Example of Building a Smart Thermostat

Let's go through the development process of building a basic smart thermostat using embedded systems and C programming.

1. Hardware Components and Setup

We will use the following hardware components for our smart thermostat:

- **Microcontroller**: **Arduino Uno** or **ESP32** (for wireless functionality)
- **Temperature Sensor**: **DHT22** or **LM35**
- **Relay**: A **5V relay module** to control a heating or cooling device
- **Display**: **LCD 16x2** or **OLED display**
- **Buttons**: Two buttons to increase or decrease the set temperature
- **Power Supply**: A 5V power supply

2. Wiring the Components

Here's how we wire the components:

- **DHT22** sensor: Connect the **VCC** and **GND** pins to the Arduino, and the **Data** pin to an available digital I/O pin (e.g., D2).
- **Relay module**: Connect the relay's control pin to a digital output pin (e.g., D3) on the Arduino. The relay will be used to control the heating or cooling system (for simplicity, we will assume it's switching a 5V fan or heater).
- **LCD**: Connect the **LCD** to the Arduino using the standard **I2C interface** (SDA, SCL pins).
- **Buttons**: Connect the buttons to digital pins (e.g., D4 and D5) for user input.

3. Firmware Design

Now, we'll design the firmware that will drive the smart thermostat. The firmware will:

- Continuously read the room temperature.
- Display the current temperature on the LCD.
- Allow the user to set a target temperature via buttons.
- Turn on/off the heating or cooling system based on the difference between the current and target temperature.

Let's begin by including the necessary libraries:

```c
#include <Wire.h>
#include <LiquidCrystal_I2C.h>
#include <DHT.h>

#define DHT_PIN 2            // Pin for the DHT22
sensor
#define RELAY_PIN 3         // Pin to control the
relay (heating/cooling system)
#define BUTTON_UP_PIN 4        // Pin for the
"Increase Temperature" button
#define BUTTON_DOWN_PIN 5      // Pin for the
"Decrease Temperature" button
```

```
DHT dht(DHT_PIN, DHT22);  // Initialize the DHT
sensor (DHT22)
LiquidCrystal_I2C  lcd(0x27,  16,  2);      //
Initialize the LCD (I2C)

int targetTemperature = 22;  // Set the default
target temperature to 22°C
int  currentTemperature  =  0;    //  Current
temperature variable
int relayState = LOW;        // Relay state (LOW
= off, HIGH = on)

void setup() {
  // Initialize the serial monitor
  Serial.begin(9600);

  // Initialize the DHT sensor and LCD
  dht.begin();
  lcd.begin(16, 2);  // 16x2 LCD

  // Set button pins as input
  pinMode(BUTTON_UP_PIN, INPUT_PULLUP);
  pinMode(BUTTON_DOWN_PIN, INPUT_PULLUP);
  pinMode(RELAY_PIN, OUTPUT);  // Set relay pin
as output

  // Display a welcome message
  lcd.setCursor(0, 0);
  lcd.print("Smart Thermostat");
```

```
  delay(2000);
}

void loop() {
  // Read temperature from the DHT sensor
  currentTemperature = dht.readTemperature();
// Get the current temperature

  // Check if the reading is valid
  if (isnan(currentTemperature)) {
    lcd.setCursor(0, 1);
    lcd.print("Error reading temp");
    return;
  }

  // Display current temperature
  lcd.setCursor(0, 1);
  lcd.print("Temp: ");
  lcd.print(currentTemperature);
  lcd.print(" C");

  // Check button presses for temperature
adjustment
  if (digitalRead(BUTTON_UP_PIN) == LOW) {
    targetTemperature++;
    delay(500);  // Debounce delay
  }

  if (digitalRead(BUTTON_DOWN_PIN) == LOW) {
```

```
    targetTemperature--;
    delay(500);  // Debounce delay
  }

  // Display the target temperature
  lcd.setCursor(0, 0);
  lcd.print("Set Temp: ");
  lcd.print(targetTemperature);
  lcd.print(" C");

  // Control the relay (heating/cooling)
  if (currentTemperature < targetTemperature - 1)
{
    relayState = HIGH;  // Turn on heating
    digitalWrite(RELAY_PIN, relayState);
  }    else    if    (currentTemperature    >
targetTemperature + 1) {
    relayState = LOW;  // Turn on cooling
    digitalWrite(RELAY_PIN, relayState);
  }

  delay(2000);  // Update every 2 seconds
}
```

Explanation of the Code:

- **DHT Sensor**: We read the current temperature using the **DHT22** sensor and display it on the LCD.

- **Target Temperature**: We set a default target temperature of **22°C**. The user can increase or decrease the target temperature using buttons connected to the Arduino.
- **Relay Control**: The relay controls the heating or cooling system. If the current temperature is below the target temperature by more than 1°C, the heating system is activated (the relay is turned on). If the current temperature is higher than the target by more than 1°C, the cooling system is activated (the relay is turned off).
- **LCD Display**: We use the **LiquidCrystal_I2C** library to display both the current temperature and the target temperature on the LCD.

4. Testing and Calibration

Once the hardware and firmware are set up, the system must be tested to ensure it works as expected:

- **Verify Sensor Accuracy**: Test the temperature sensor by comparing its readings with a known accurate thermometer. Calibrate the sensor if necessary.
- **Test Relay Control**: Ensure that the relay correctly switches on and off based on the temperature difference.
- **Button Functionality**: Ensure that the buttons accurately adjust the target temperature and that the system responds accordingly.

5. Enhancements and Future Features

Once the basic smart thermostat is working, there are many potential enhancements:

- **Wi-Fi Connectivity**: Implement wireless communication using an **ESP32** or **ESP8266** so users can control the thermostat remotely via a smartphone app or web interface.
- **Scheduling**: Allow users to set different target temperatures at different times of day (e.g., lower temperatures at night).
- **Energy Monitoring**: Track and display energy consumption based on the heating/cooling system's operation.
- **Voice Control**: Integrate with voice assistants like **Amazon Alexa** or **Google Assistant** for voice-based control.

Conclusion

In this chapter, we went through the process of designing and developing a basic **smart thermostat** using embedded systems and C programming. We discussed the hardware components needed, such as the temperature sensor, relay, display, and buttons, and walked through the firmware development to control the thermostat's operation. By following this step-by-step guide, you can build your own smart home device and customize it further based on your needs. This case study illustrates the power of embedded systems in creating smart devices that can improve comfort and energy efficiency in a home environment.

CHAPTER 24

REAL-WORLD APPLICATION: INDUSTRIAL AUTOMATION

Using Embedded Systems for Industrial Automation

Industrial automation is the use of control systems, such as **PLCs (Programmable Logic Controllers)**, **sensors**, and **actuators**, to automate industrial processes. Embedded systems play a crucial role in industrial automation, as they provide the intelligence, control, and communication necessary to ensure efficient and reliable operation. In this chapter, we will explore how embedded systems are applied in industrial automation, the key components involved, and how to interface with sensors, actuators, and PLCs to create automated systems.

1. What is Industrial Automation?

Industrial automation refers to the use of technology to control equipment, processes, and systems in manufacturing and production environments. The goal of industrial automation is to improve efficiency, reduce human intervention, enhance safety, and optimize production processes. Embedded systems are central to this process, providing the necessary control, monitoring, and communication capabilities.

Some common applications of industrial automation include:

- **Assembly lines**: Automated control of manufacturing processes.
- **Robot control**: Precision control of robotic arms or mobile robots.
- **Process control**: Monitoring and adjusting variables such as temperature, pressure, or flow rate in chemical or manufacturing plants.
- **Machine monitoring**: Continuous tracking of equipment performance, wear, and failures.

2. Role of Embedded Systems in Industrial Automation

Embedded systems in industrial automation typically serve three primary functions:

1. **Control**: Embedded systems control machinery, processes, and equipment by processing input signals from sensors and generating appropriate output signals for actuators.

2. **Monitoring**: Embedded systems monitor the status of equipment and processes, collecting data from sensors and feeding this information to control systems or human operators.
3. **Communication**: Embedded systems enable communication between various industrial devices, systems, and networks, allowing for remote control, data acquisition, and integration with higher-level systems like SCADA (Supervisory Control and Data Acquisition).

Embedded systems are designed to be reliable, real-time, and capable of withstanding harsh industrial environments, including exposure to high temperatures, humidity, and electromagnetic interference.

Interfacing with Sensors, Actuators, and PLCs

In industrial automation, embedded systems need to interface with various components, including **sensors**, **actuators**, and **PLCs**, to gather data and control the system effectively.

1. Sensors in Industrial Automation

Sensors are used to measure physical parameters like temperature, pressure, humidity, speed, or proximity. The embedded system collects data from these sensors, processes it, and makes decisions based on the readings. Sensors provide critical feedback for controlling processes in real-time.

Common types of sensors used in industrial automation include:

- **Temperature Sensors**: Used to measure the temperature of machines or environments. Examples include **thermocouples** or **RTDs (resistance temperature detectors)**.
- **Proximity Sensors**: Used to detect the presence of objects or components in a system. Examples include **inductive**, **capacitive**, or **ultrasonic** sensors.
- **Pressure Sensors**: Measure the pressure of fluids or gases in pipes, tanks, or pumps.
- **Flow Sensors**: Monitor the flow of liquids or gases in industrial systems.
- **Position Sensors**: Used in robotic systems or conveyor belts to track the position of objects or tools.

Example: Interfacing a Temperature Sensor

In an industrial system, temperature is often a critical parameter. Here's how you would interface a **LM35 temperature sensor** with an embedded system to monitor the temperature:

```c
#define TEMPERATURE_SENSOR_PIN A0 // LM35 connected to analog pin A0

void setup() {
  Serial.begin(9600);
}

void loop() {
  int sensorValue = analogRead(TEMPERATURE_SENSOR_PIN); // Read the sensor value
  float voltage = sensorValue * (5.0 / 1023.0); // Convert analog value to voltage
  float temperature = voltage * 100; // Convert voltage to temperature in Celsius

  Serial.print("Temperature: ");
  Serial.print(temperature);
  Serial.println(" C");

  delay(1000); // Wait for 1 second before taking another reading
}
```

Explanation:

- The **LM35** sensor provides an output that is proportional to the temperature. In this case, it outputs 10 mV per degree Celsius.
- The **analogRead()** function reads the analog voltage output from the sensor, and we convert this value into a temperature in Celsius.

2. Actuators in Industrial Automation

Actuators are used to perform physical actions based on the control signals provided by the embedded system. Actuators convert electrical signals into mechanical movement, such as moving a robotic arm, opening a valve, or starting a motor.

Common types of actuators include:

- **Motors**: Used to drive mechanical movements, such as motors in conveyor belts, robotic arms, or pumps.
- **Valves**: Control the flow of liquids or gases in industrial systems.
- **Relays**: Control high-power devices, such as lights, motors, or heating elements, based on the control signals from the embedded system.
- **Solenoids**: Used to control mechanical movements by converting electrical energy into linear motion.

Example: Controlling a Motor with an Embedded System

Here's an example of controlling a DC motor using a relay. The motor will turn on when the temperature exceeds a certain threshold.

```c
#define RELAY_PIN 3
#define TEMPERATURE_SENSOR_PIN A0

void setup() {
  pinMode(RELAY_PIN, OUTPUT);
  Serial.begin(9600);
}

void loop() {
  int sensorValue = analogRead(TEMPERATURE_SENSOR_PIN);  // Read the temperature sensor value
  float voltage = sensorValue * (5.0 / 1023.0);
  float temperature = voltage * 100;  // Convert voltage to temperature in Celsius

  // Print the temperature
  Serial.print("Temperature: ");
  Serial.print(temperature);
  Serial.println(" C");
```

```
  if (temperature > 30) {   // If temperature
exceeds 30°C
    digitalWrite(RELAY_PIN, HIGH);   // Turn on
the motor
  } else {
    digitalWrite(RELAY_PIN, LOW);   // Turn off
the motor
  }

  delay(1000);   // Wait for 1 second before
taking another reading
}
```

Explanation:

- This example controls a **DC motor** using a **relay**. If the temperature exceeds 30°C, the motor is activated (relay switched on).
- The **analogRead()** function reads the sensor value, and based on the temperature, the motor is either turned on or off.

3. Interfacing with PLCs (Programmable Logic Controllers)

In industrial automation, **PLCs** are often used to control machinery and processes. PLCs offer a reliable, rugged, and real-time control solution for industrial environments.

Embedded systems can interface with PLCs via various communication protocols such as **Modbus**, **PROFIBUS**, or **Ethernet/IP**.

- **Modbus**: A widely used communication protocol in industrial automation. It allows embedded systems to exchange data with PLCs over serial or TCP/IP networks.
- **PROFIBUS**: A fieldbus standard used for communication between automation devices, including PLCs, sensors, and actuators.
- **Ethernet/IP**: An industrial Ethernet protocol that enables real-time data exchange between embedded systems, PLCs, and other devices.

Example: Interfacing an Embedded System with a PLC using Modbus RTU

Here's an example of how an embedded system (e.g., Arduino) can communicate with a PLC using **Modbus RTU** over a serial interface. This example uses the **ModbusMaster** library to send and receive data from the PLC.

```c
#include <ModbusMaster.h>
```

```
ModbusMaster node;

void setup() {
  Serial.begin(9600);
  node.begin(1, Serial);   // Initialize Modbus
communication with slave ID 1
}

void loop() {
  uint8_t result;
  result = node.readHoldingRegisters(0x00, 2);
// Read two holding registers (address 0x00)

  if (result == node.ku8MBSuccess) {
    int temperature = node.getResponseBuffer(0);
// Get the value from the first register
    Serial.print("Temperature: ");
    Serial.println(temperature);
  }

  delay(1000);  // Wait for 1 second before the
next request
}
```

Explanation:

- The **ModbusMaster** library allows the Arduino to communicate with a Modbus-compatible PLC using a **serial interface**.

- The system reads the temperature (holding register 0x00) from the PLC and displays it on the serial monitor.

Conclusion

In this chapter, we explored how embedded systems are used in **industrial automation** to monitor, control, and communicate with various devices and systems. We covered the role of **sensors**, **actuators**, and **PLCs** in industrial applications, and provided practical examples of how embedded systems interface with these components. By leveraging embedded systems, industrial automation can be made more efficient, reliable, and responsive, enabling real-time control and data-driven decision-making. As industries continue to adopt IoT and smart technologies, embedded systems will remain at the core of automated systems, driving innovation in manufacturing, process control, and robotics.

CHAPTER 25

DATA LOGGING AND DATA STORAGE IN EMBEDDED SYSTEMS

Techniques for Logging Data on Embedded Systems

Data logging is an essential feature of many embedded systems, where the system is tasked with collecting, storing, and possibly transmitting data for later analysis or processing. Embedded systems often need to log data from sensors, user inputs, or other sources for long periods, without direct human intervention. The logged data could be anything from environmental measurements (temperature, humidity, etc.) to event logs in industrial or automotive systems.

In this chapter, we will explore the techniques used for logging data in embedded systems, focusing on local storage methods using **SD cards**, **EEPROM**, and other storage media. We will also discuss how to ensure reliable and efficient data logging, particularly in systems with limited resources.

1. Why Data Logging is Important in Embedded Systems

Data logging is used in various applications, including:

- **Environmental monitoring**: Logging temperature, humidity, air quality, etc., for agriculture, healthcare, and weather stations.
- **Industrial systems**: Monitoring machinery performance, sensor readings, or production data.
- **Automotive**: Collecting vehicle diagnostic data or telemetry for fleet management.
- **IoT**: Collecting data from remote sensors or devices and sending it for analysis or cloud storage.

The primary goal of data logging in embedded systems is to ensure that data is collected accurately, stored efficiently, and is accessible for later use. However, data logging in embedded systems must also be performed in an efficient manner that does not compromise system performance or use excessive power.

Techniques for Data Logging

There are several methods of logging data in embedded systems, depending on the size of data, the available resources, and the use case.

1. **Internal Memory Logging**:
   - In small-scale embedded systems, it may be possible to log data directly into the internal memory (e.g., SRAM, flash). This method is suitable for storing small amounts of data.
   - **Limitation**: Internal memory in microcontrollers is usually small and may not support long-term data storage for larger projects.
2. **External Memory Logging**:
   - For larger data logging requirements, external storage devices like **SD cards**, **EEPROMs**, or **flash memory** are commonly used. These devices offer higher storage capacity and can be accessed easily through standard interfaces like SPI or I2C.

2. Using External Storage for Data Logging

External storage options like **SD cards** and **EEPROM** are popular choices for embedded systems that need to log data over extended periods. Let's explore how these devices are used in embedded systems.

2.1 SD Cards for Data Logging

SD cards are commonly used in embedded systems because they provide a significant amount of storage (ranging from several MB to GBs) and are easy to interface with using common communication protocols like **SPI**.

How SD Card Data Logging Works:

- An SD card is interfaced with the microcontroller via the **SPI** interface.
- The microcontroller can write data to the SD card in a **text**, **binary**, or **CSV** format, depending on the application.
- The data is typically written to files, and the logging system needs to manage file creation, data writing, and error handling.

Advantages:

- High storage capacity.
- Standardized file system (FAT16, FAT32) makes it easy to store and retrieve data.
- Low cost and widely available.

Example: Logging Temperature Data to an SD Card

```c
#include <SPI.h>
#include <SD.h>
#include <DHT.h>
```

```
#define DHTPIN 2     // Pin connected to the DHT22
sensor
#define DHTTYPE DHT22  // DHT 22 (AM2302)

DHT dht(DHTPIN, DHTTYPE);
File dataFile;

void setup() {
  Serial.begin(9600);

  if (!SD.begin(4)) {   // Initialize SD card at
pin 4
    Serial.println("SD    card    initialization
failed!");
    return;
  }

  Serial.println("SD card initialized.");
  dht.begin();

  // Open the file for writing
  dataFile = SD.open("datalog.txt", FILE_WRITE);
  if (dataFile) {
    dataFile.println("Temperature, Humidity");
    dataFile.close();
  } else {
    Serial.println("Error opening datalog.txt");
  }
```

```
}

void loop() {
  float temperature = dht.readTemperature();
  float humidity = dht.readHumidity();

  if (isnan(temperature) || isnan(humidity)) {
    Serial.println("Failed  to  read  from  DHT
sensor!");
    return;
  }

  // Open the file again for appending data
  dataFile = SD.open("datalog.txt", FILE_WRITE);
  if (dataFile) {
    dataFile.print(temperature);
    dataFile.print(", ");
    dataFile.println(humidity);
    dataFile.close();
  } else {
    Serial.println("Error opening datalog.txt");
  }

  delay(2000);  // Log data every 2 seconds
}
```

Explanation:

- We use the **DHT22** sensor to read the temperature and humidity.
- Data is logged to the **SD card** in CSV format, which allows easy processing and analysis of data.
- The program appends data to the file every 2 seconds.

2.2 EEPROM for Data Logging

EEPROM (Electrically Erasable Programmable Read-Only Memory) is a type of non-volatile memory used for storing small amounts of data that need to persist even when the system is powered off. Embedded systems often use **external EEPROM** for data logging in systems with limited memory or where the data to be stored is small in size.

How EEPROM Data Logging Works:

- EEPROM is typically accessed via **I2C** or **SPI** interfaces.
- It is suitable for logging small amounts of data, such as settings or sensor readings, but is not ideal for large-scale data logging due to its limited storage capacity (usually in the range of kilobytes).

Advantages:

- Retains data when power is lost.

- Can be accessed at the byte level, making it easy to store individual data points.
- More energy-efficient than SD cards for small data logging tasks.

Example: Logging Data to EEPROM

```
c

#include <Wire.h>
#include <EEPROM.h>
#include <DHT.h>

#define DHTPIN 2     // Pin connected to the DHT22
sensor
#define DHTTYPE DHT22  // DHT 22 (AM2302)

DHT dht(DHTPIN, DHTTYPE);

int address = 0;  // EEPROM address for storing
data

void setup() {
  Serial.begin(9600);
  dht.begin();
}

void loop() {
  float temperature = dht.readTemperature();
```

```
  float humidity = dht.readHumidity();

  if (isnan(temperature) || isnan(humidity)) {
    Serial.println("Failed to read from DHT sensor!");
    return;
  }

  // Store data in EEPROM
  EEPROM.write(address, temperature);  // Store temperature at the current address
  address++;  // Move to the next memory location
  EEPROM.write(address, humidity);  // Store humidity at the next address
  address++;

  // Display logged data
  Serial.print("Temperature: ");
  Serial.print(temperature);
  Serial.print(" Humidity: ");
  Serial.println(humidity);

  delay(2000);  // Log data every 2 seconds
}
```

Explanation:

- This example logs **temperature** and **humidity** data from the **DHT22** sensor into **EEPROM** memory.

- Data is stored at consecutive memory locations in EEPROM, and the `address` is incremented after each write.
- **EEPROM** is ideal for small-scale data storage and logging, but limited in capacity compared to SD cards.

3. Data Logging Best Practices

When implementing data logging in embedded systems, there are several best practices to consider:

1. **Data Integrity**:
   - Use **checksums** or **hashes** to ensure the integrity of the data being written to storage.
   - Implement error handling mechanisms to detect and recover from write failures.
2. **Power Fail Protection**:
   - In the event of a power failure, data might be lost if not properly written to storage. Use techniques such as writing data periodically or using **capacitors** to provide enough time to save the data during an unexpected shutdown.
3. **Efficient Data Storage**:
   - For large-scale data logging, it's important to minimize the amount of data stored, especially on devices with limited storage. **Data compression**

algorithms or **buffering** data before writing to storage can help.

- Consider logging data in smaller, discrete chunks instead of continuously writing to reduce wear on storage media, especially for **SD cards**.

4. **Data Retrieval**:
   - Ensure that the stored data is in a format that is easy to retrieve and process (e.g., CSV, JSON).
   - Implement a user-friendly interface (e.g., a web server or Bluetooth) to access the logged data remotely.

Conclusion

Data logging is a fundamental feature of many embedded systems, enabling devices to collect, store, and retrieve important information for analysis and control. By using external storage devices such as **SD cards** or **EEPROM**, embedded systems can store large or small amounts of data efficiently and reliably. By following best practices in data integrity, power fail protection, and efficient storage, developers can create systems that accurately log and store data over long periods. Data logging is a crucial aspect of applications in fields such as environmental monitoring, industrial automation, healthcare, and IoT, helping systems track performance, gather statistics, and make data-driven decisions.

CHAPTER 26

BUILDING A COMPLETE EMBEDDED SYSTEM APPLICATION

Integrating Hardware and Software in an Embedded System

The process of building an embedded system involves integrating both hardware and software to create a fully functional application. This chapter will guide you through the process of developing a complete embedded system application, from hardware design to software development and testing.

Embedded systems are often highly specialized and designed for specific tasks, which means the integration of hardware and software must be efficient, reliable, and optimized for the given resources. Successful embedded system development requires careful attention to both the hardware components (microcontrollers, sensors, actuators) and the software running on the system.

1. Key Stages in Developing an Embedded System Application

To build a complete embedded system application, the development process can be broken down into several stages:

1. **System Design and Requirements**: Define the application's goals, the required hardware components, and the functionality of the system.
2. **Hardware Selection and Design**: Choose the microcontroller, sensors, actuators, and other peripherals based on the system's needs.
3. **Software Development**: Write firmware to control the hardware, implement logic, and ensure reliable operation.
4. **Testing and Debugging**: Test the embedded system thoroughly to ensure that the hardware and software work together as expected.
5. **Deployment and Maintenance**: Deploy the system to the target environment and monitor its performance, making updates or fixes when necessary.

2. Hardware and Software Integration in Embedded Systems

Hardware and software need to be tightly coupled to ensure that they function together effectively. Below are the key integration points when developing an embedded system application.

1. **Microcontroller and Peripherals**:
   - The **microcontroller** is the brain of the embedded system, and it interacts with sensors and actuators to perform tasks.
   - **Interfacing hardware components** like sensors, motors, relays, displays, and communication modules (e.g., Wi-Fi, Bluetooth) requires programming the microcontroller's I/O pins and communication protocols.
   - Use **drivers** or **libraries** to simplify interfacing with peripherals, such as sensors and displays.
2. **Firmware Development**:
   - Firmware is the software that runs on the microcontroller, enabling it to interact with hardware and control the system.
   - The firmware needs to manage real-time operations, handle sensor readings, and control actuators based on inputs.
   - Embedded systems often use **interrupts** and **timers** to respond to real-time events and manage tasks in a predictable manner.
3. **Real-Time Constraints**:
   - Many embedded systems have real-time requirements, meaning that certain operations must be completed within specific time limits

(e.g., reading sensor data every second, activating a relay within milliseconds).

- **RTOS (Real-Time Operating Systems)** may be used to manage these constraints and allocate resources effectively, but in simpler systems, **bare-metal programming** (without an operating system) is often sufficient.

3. Developing a Final Embedded Application from Start to Finish

Let's walk through the steps of developing a complete embedded system application. For this example, we will create a **smart door lock system** using a microcontroller (e.g., Arduino) that will interface with a **fingerprint sensor** for authentication and a **servo motor** for locking and unlocking the door.

3.1 System Design and Requirements

- **Goal**: Design a system that authenticates a user via a fingerprint scanner and then controls a servo motor to lock or unlock a door.
- **Components**:
  - **Microcontroller**: Arduino Uno or similar.
  - **Fingerprint Sensor**: **R305 Fingerprint Sensor** for user authentication.
  - **Servo Motor**: To control the locking mechanism.

- **Button**: For manual override of the lock (optional).
- **Power Supply**: To power the system.
- **Communication Interface**: Serial communication between the Arduino and the fingerprint sensor.

3.2 Hardware Setup

- **Fingerprint Sensor**: The sensor will be connected to the Arduino using **serial communication** (TX/RX pins).
- **Servo Motor**: The servo motor will be connected to one of the PWM-capable pins on the Arduino (e.g., Pin 9).
- **Button**: The button will be connected to a digital I/O pin on the Arduino for manual override (optional).

3.3 Writing the Firmware

Here's a simple implementation of the firmware that will handle the sensor input, verify the fingerprint, and control the servo motor.

c

```
#include <Adafruit_Fingerprint.h>
#include <Servo.h>

// Pin definitions
```

```
#define BUTTON_PIN 2
#define SERVO_PIN 9

// Initialize servo and fingerprint sensor
Servo myservo;
SoftwareSerial mySerial(10, 11); // RX, TX for
fingerprint sensor
Adafruit_Fingerprint          finger          =
Adafruit_Fingerprint(&mySerial);

int lockPosition = 0;  // Closed position of the
lock
int unlockPosition = 90;  // Open position of the
lock

void setup() {
  Serial.begin(9600);       //    Start    serial
communication
  myservo.attach(SERVO_PIN);  // Attach the servo
to pin 9
  pinMode(BUTTON_PIN,  INPUT_PULLUP);    //   Set
button pin as input

  if (finger.begin()) {
    Serial.println("Fingerprint            sensor
initialized.");
  } else {
    Serial.println("Fingerprint    sensor    not
detected!");
```

```
    while (1);
  }

  myservo.write(lockPosition);    // Initially,
lock the door
  delay(1000);
}

void loop() {
  if (digitalRead(BUTTON_PIN) == LOW) {
    // Manual override: If the button is pressed,
unlock the door
    myservo.write(unlockPosition);    // Unlock
the door
    delay(3000);  // Wait for 3 seconds and then
lock the door again
    myservo.write(lockPosition);    // Lock the
door
    delay(1000);
  }

  getFingerprint();
}

void getFingerprint() {
  int ret = finger.getImage();
  if (ret != FINGERPRINT_OK) {
    Serial.println("Failed to read fingerprint
image.");
```

```
    return;
  }

  ret = finger.image2Tz();
  if (ret != FINGERPRINT_OK) {
    Serial.println("Failed to convert image.");
    return;
  }

  ret = finger.fingerSearch();
  if (ret == FINGERPRINT_OK) {
    Serial.println("Fingerprint recognized.");
    myservo.write(unlockPosition);    // Unlock
the door
    delay(5000);  // Keep the door unlocked for
5 seconds
    myservo.write(lockPosition);    // Lock the
door
  } else {
    Serial.println("Fingerprint                not
recognized.");
  }
}
```

Explanation:

- The **Adafruit Fingerprint** library is used to interface with the fingerprint sensor.

- The **Servo** library is used to control the servo motor that locks and unlocks the door.
- The program first waits for a valid fingerprint scan. If recognized, the servo moves to the unlock position, and the door stays unlocked for 5 seconds before relocking.
- The button provides a manual override to unlock the door for 3 seconds.

3.4 Testing and Debugging

Once the hardware is set up and the firmware is loaded onto the microcontroller, the system should be tested as follows:

1. Verify that the **fingerprint sensor** reads and processes fingerprints correctly.
2. Test the **servo motor** to ensure that it moves to the correct position for locking and unlocking the door.
3. Test the **manual override button** to ensure that the door can be unlocked manually.
4. Test error handling for failed fingerprint scans.

If any part of the system does not work as expected, use debugging tools such as **serial output** or a **logic analyzer** to troubleshoot and identify issues.

3.5 Deployment and Maintenance

Once the system has been tested and is working reliably, it can be deployed to the final application environment (e.g., a smart home or office). Periodically, the fingerprint database may need to be updated or additional users added.

- **Firmware updates** can be done via **OTA** (Over-the-Air) or by re-flashing the microcontroller.
- If the fingerprint sensor or servo motor fails, **diagnostic messages** can be displayed via the **serial monitor** or through a **status LED**.
- **Backup mechanisms** can be implemented for user data (e.g., store fingerprint templates in non-volatile memory).

Conclusion

In this chapter, we walked through the process of building a complete embedded system application: a **smart door lock** using a **fingerprint sensor** and a **servo motor**. We discussed the key steps involved in integrating hardware and software, from defining system requirements and designing the hardware to writing firmware, testing, and deployment. Building complete embedded applications requires

A network error occurred. Please check your connection and try again. If this issue persists please contact us through our help center at help.openai.com.

CHAPTER 27

FUTURE TRENDS IN EMBEDDED SYSTEMS DEVELOPMENT

Trends in Embedded Systems (IoT, Edge Computing, AI Integration)

Embedded systems have evolved significantly over the years, and their role in modern technology continues to expand. With the growing need for intelligent, efficient, and connected devices, several major trends are shaping the future of embedded systems. In this chapter, we will explore the key trends in embedded systems development, including the Internet of Things (IoT), edge computing, and the integration of artificial intelligence (AI).

1. The Internet of Things (IoT) and Embedded Systems

The **Internet of Things (IoT)** refers to the network of physical devices embedded with sensors, software, and other technologies that enable them to connect and exchange data with other devices and systems over the internet. IoT is transforming industries, from home automation to healthcare, agriculture, and industrial applications, by enabling smart devices that can collect, process, and share data in real-time.

Key Factors Driving IoT in Embedded Systems:

- **Connectivity**: As more devices become connected, embedded systems must support multiple communication protocols (e.g., Wi-Fi, Bluetooth, Zigbee, LoRaWAN, and 5G) to interact with other IoT devices and networks.
- **Low Power Consumption**: IoT devices often operate in remote or battery-powered environments, requiring embedded systems to be highly efficient in terms of energy consumption.
- **Security**: IoT systems are vulnerable to cyberattacks, making security a critical concern. Embedded systems must integrate encryption, authentication, and secure communication protocols to protect data and devices.
- **Data Processing**: IoT devices generate massive amounts of data, which must be processed and analyzed either on the device itself or transmitted to cloud-based platforms for further processing.

Example: In a **smart home** application, embedded systems in thermostats, lights, and security cameras are connected via IoT to enable users to control their home remotely using a smartphone app. These systems collect data (e.g., temperature, motion) and share it with a central platform for analysis and action.

2. Edge Computing in Embedded Systems

Edge computing refers to the practice of processing data closer to its source (on the edge of the network) rather than transmitting it to centralized cloud servers. This approach is particularly important for embedded systems, as it helps reduce latency, save bandwidth, and enable real-time processing.

In the context of embedded systems, edge computing involves using microcontrollers, sensors, and actuators to perform data processing directly on the device or at a nearby gateway rather than relying solely on cloud-based services.

Benefits of Edge Computing in Embedded Systems:

- **Reduced Latency**: By processing data locally, edge computing minimizes the time it takes for a system to respond to real-world inputs, making it ideal for time-sensitive applications like autonomous vehicles or industrial control systems.
- **Bandwidth Efficiency**: Transmitting large amounts of raw data to the cloud can be inefficient and costly. Edge

computing enables embedded systems to preprocess or filter data before sending only relevant information to the cloud, reducing network bandwidth usage.

- **Improved Privacy and Security**: Sensitive data can be processed locally, reducing the risk of data exposure while in transit to cloud servers. This is particularly important in healthcare, finance, and other privacy-sensitive industries.

Example: In an industrial setting, edge computing is used for predictive maintenance. Sensors on machines collect data (e.g., vibration, temperature) and analyze it locally to detect potential issues. If an anomaly is detected, the embedded system can trigger an alert without needing to send all the data to the cloud.

3. Artificial Intelligence (AI) Integration in Embedded Systems

The integration of **Artificial Intelligence (AI)** into embedded systems is one of the most transformative trends in embedded systems development. AI and machine learning (ML) algorithms enable embedded systems to learn from data, make decisions autonomously, and adapt to changing environments.

AI and ML in Embedded Systems:

- **AI at the Edge**: The combination of edge computing and AI allows embedded systems to perform complex data analysis locally, enabling devices to make intelligent decisions without relying on cloud-based AI models. This is often referred to as **AI on the edge**.
- **Voice and Image Recognition**: AI-powered embedded systems are increasingly being used in applications that require speech or image recognition, such as voice assistants (e.g., Amazon Alexa) or security cameras with facial recognition.
- **Predictive Analytics**: AI models in embedded systems can analyze sensor data in real-time to predict future events or trends. For example, an embedded system in a car could predict potential engine failures by analyzing data from various sensors.

Challenges of AI Integration in Embedded Systems:

- **Processing Power**: AI algorithms, particularly deep learning models, require significant computational resources. Embedded systems with limited processing power must use efficient algorithms or offload processing to more powerful devices (e.g., edge gateways or cloud platforms).
- **Power Consumption**: Running AI algorithms on embedded systems, especially in battery-powered

devices, can be resource-intensive. Optimizing AI models for power efficiency is essential.

- **Data Quality and Training**: AI systems require high-quality, well-labeled data for training. In embedded systems, collecting sufficient data in real-world conditions can be challenging.

Example: In **smart cameras**, embedded systems with AI capabilities use image recognition to detect faces, movements, or specific objects. The system processes the video feed locally on the camera before sending relevant data to a cloud server or taking action, such as alerting a user or activating a security alarm.

Preparing for Future Developments in Embedded Systems

As the embedded systems landscape continues to evolve, it is crucial for developers and engineers to stay up to date with emerging trends and technologies. Here are a few ways to prepare for future developments in embedded systems:

1. Embrace New Connectivity Standards:

- With the rise of IoT, new connectivity standards such as **5G**, **LoRaWAN**, and **Zigbee** are becoming more prevalent. These technologies enable high-speed, long-range, and low-power communication between embedded devices, opening up new possibilities for industrial IoT, smart cities, and consumer applications.

2. Explore AI and Machine Learning:

- As AI integration in embedded systems grows, developers should familiarize themselves with machine learning frameworks and tools, such as **TensorFlow Lite** and **Edge Impulse**, which are optimized for low-power embedded devices. AI and ML skills will be valuable as more embedded systems are designed to perform intelligent tasks.

3. Invest in Edge Computing Solutions:

- Edge computing is expected to play a major role in future embedded systems, especially in applications requiring real-time decision-making. Developers should explore edge AI platforms and learn how to design systems that process data locally while communicating with cloud platforms when needed.

4. Prioritize Security:

- As more devices become connected, cybersecurity will remain a top concern. Developers must stay updated on the latest security protocols and standards for embedded systems, including **secure boot**, **encryption**, **identity**

management, and **secure communication** protocols like **TLS** and **VPNs**.

5. Optimize for Energy Efficiency:

- With the growing demand for battery-powered devices, energy efficiency will be a critical focus. Developers should optimize software for low power consumption, explore low-power wireless communication technologies, and make use of hardware features like low-power modes.

6. Adopt Modular and Scalable Designs:

- As embedded systems become more complex and interconnected, modularity and scalability will be essential. Designing systems that can be easily upgraded, reconfigured, or expanded will ensure that devices can adapt to new requirements and use cases.

Conclusion

The future of embedded systems is deeply intertwined with the rise of **IoT**, **edge computing**, and **AI**. As more devices become interconnected, capable of real-time decision-making, and smarter through AI, embedded systems will become even more integrated into daily life. By staying informed and adopting the latest technologies, embedded systems developers will be well-prepared for the evolving landscape of embedded applications, from industrial automation and smart cities to personal devices and healthcare. The next generation of embedded systems will require a blend of creativity, technical expertise, and a forward-thinking approach to meet the growing demand for smarter, more efficient, and more secure devices.

www.ingramcontent.com/pod-product-compliance
Lightning Source LLC
LaVergne TN
LVHW051436050326
832903LV00030BD/3120

* 9 7 9 8 3 1 4 9 6 8 6 4 2 *